The Savvy Student's Guide to Online Learning

The Savvy Student's Guide to Online Learning prepares students of all kinds for contemporary online learning. While technologies and formats vary, this book serves as an authoritative resource for any student enrolling in an online degree program or taking an online course.

Topics covered include:

- How to become a great online student
- Creating an online presence
- Interaction and communication techniques
- Online group projects and individual work
- Technological requirements and how to get technical support
- Online classroom "netiquette" and time management

The authors, both experts in online education, introduce the information and skills required of successful online students to navigate this new learning landscape with confidence. A highly useful companion website provides video presentations that explain the different types of online learning as well as a real online course with activities for students to practice and interact with other learners around the world.

Kristen Sosulski is the Director of the Center for Innovation in Teaching and Learning and clinical assistant professor of information systems at New York University, Stern. She has her Ed.D. from Columbia University Teachers College.

Ted Bongiovanni is the Director of the New York University School of Continuing and Professional Studies Office of Distance Learning and teaches online courses in research methods and project management.

The Savvy Student's Guide to Online Learning

Kristen Sosulski
Ted Bongiovanni

Routledge
Taylor & Francis Group

NEW YORK AND LONDON

Please visit the book's companion website at
http://savvyonlinestudent.com

First published 2013
by Routledge
711 Third Avenue, New York, NY 10017

Simultaneously published in the UK
by Routledge
2 Park Square, Milton Park, Abingdon, Oxon OX14 4RN

Routledge is an imprint of the Taylor & Francis Group, an informa business

Library of Congress Cataloging in Publication Data
  Sosulski, Kristen.
  The savvy student's guide to online learning: by Kristen Sosulski and
  Ted Bongiovanni.
  p. cm.
  Includes bibliographical references and index.
  1. Distance education—Computer-assisted instruction. 2. Internet in
  education. I. Bongiovanni, Ted. II. Title.
  LC5803.C65S67 2013
  371.33'44678—dc23
  2012046745

ISBN: 978-0-415-65597-2 (hbk)
ISBN: 978-0-415-65598-9 (pbk)
ISBN: 978-0-203-07825-9 (ebk)

Typeset in Helvetica Neue and Optima
by Florence Production Ltd, Stoodleigh, Devon, UK

SUSTAINABLE
FORESTRY
INITIATIVE

Certified Sourcing
www.sfiprogram.org
SFI-00555
The SFI label applies to the text stock.

Printed and bound in the United States of America by
Walsworth Publishing Company, Marceline, MO.

Contents

Preface

We wrote this book after years of teaching online courses and designing online orientations for college students. This is a book for students, by two teachers, and life long learners. In it, we proclaim that online learning is learning. Knowing how to learn online is an essential skill today. Just because we are able to learn in other contexts that does not mean that we are savvy about learning online. It's similar in many ways, but different in others.

There have never been more opportunities to learn online. Many universities offer open courses such as Coursera, EdX, Udacity. Signing up for online courses is easy. Staying on track, managing your time, and being diligent is much more difficult. This guide simplifies and demystifies those seemingly straightforward tasks.

We found that students need more preparation for taking an online course, or enrolling in a program. Colleges and universities make a good effort, but still don't do enough. This book supplements online student orientations. It is filled with opportunities to practice using new tools. We show students what is different about online learning as well as explain what is similar or the same. Email your critiques, feedback and ideas to ideas@savvyonlinestudent.com.

Kristen Sosulski

There are very few times in life when you can make choices concerning who you work with and when. I've had the privilege of working with Ted in a variety of contexts. I asked Ted to write this book with me as a testament to our synergies as educators and passion for designing engaging learning experiences. When I think of learning, what immediately comes to mind is what the student is doing, rather than the instructor. This student-centered mindset, one that Ted shares with me (and reminds me of when I deviate) has guided my career as a professor.

Ted Bongiovanni

When Kristen asked me to write this book with her I knew there could only be one answer—an emphatic yes. We started working together over 10 years ago at Columbia University's Center for New Media Teaching and Learning (CCNMTL) and continue to this day at New York University (NYU). We share much of the same educational DNA: a strong belief in the importance of putting learning first, and technology second, an emphasis on doing, and a passion for learning new things. She is a focused, dedicated, and wonderfully enthusiastic collaborator. I am also honored to count her as a friend.

I would also like to recognize and thank the team at the NYU-SCPS Office of Distance Learning. Clement Wu, Deepa Rao, Bancha Srikacha, Jill Roter, Bobby Aviles, and Mary Ann Mazzella.

Finally, I am incredibly grateful to my spouse, Deb Waldman, for the support, encouragement, and time she gave me to write this book.

Acknowledgments

We are incredibly grateful to all the faculty and students that have contributed to this book whether in idea or actual content. Harry Chernoff planted the seed to write this book. We thought it was a terrific idea and went running to Routledge. Alex Masulis was there eager to hear the new idea and has been supportive throughout the process. Lisa Springer read many early versions of chapters and the entire manuscript and helped shape the book. Sue Woodman made our copy much clearer and readable. Sachin Bagri, Won Jun Lee, Yona Jean-Pierre, and Rob Steiner all provided helpful feedback on chapters. A special thanks to Steven Goss for designing the cover and all the hand drawn illustrations.

Finally, we'd like to thank all that have supported our ambition to write this book and to those teachers that have taught us.

Introduction

According to the Babson Survey Research Group, over 6.1 million students were taking at least one online course during the fall 2010 term, an increase of 560,000 students over the previous year. Since then, millions more have enrolled in Massive Online Open Courses (MOOCs), like Stanford University's "Artificial Intelligence" course. If you have ever googled for information, you have learned something *online* even if was just from reading an article or watching a video. But online courses are much more than just *reading* content or watching videos. They are rich experiences where you engage with the content, hold conversations with instructors and other students, and learn in online social spaces where students participate in simulations, play games, and join virtual teams to collaborate on projects.

You might think that an online class is about a professor lecturing on a subject and serving as the only source for answers. This is a common misconception. In fact, the class is much less centered on the professor and is more centered on you the student. Instead of a physical classroom a digital learning environment becomes your learning hub. There, you'll access the course syllabus and class materials, complete assignments, take tests, participate in discussions, meet your peers, and join a lively community of learners.

Who's This Book For?

- Students 'enrolled' in an online course or program in a college or university, open or paid courses.

- Students considering enrolling in an online course or a degree program.

- Academic program directors, chairs, administrators, and faculty who lead online degree programs. This book can serve as an orientation to the online learning process.

- Individuals involved in online teaching and training at all levels including (1) Online teachers (K–12 level), teaching assistants, and professors; (2) Educational technologists who train instructors how to teach online; and (3) Undergraduate and graduate educational technology students looking to work in the area of distance education.

What's Ahead?

In Chapters 1 and 2 we discuss online course expectations and build on your experience as a classroom learner. The tools for communication and collaboration are presented and explained. Finally, we help you build your online learning toolkit.

In Chapters 3 and 4 you'll learn how to create your online presence, make a positive impression, and form lasting relationships with your peers and instructors.

In Chapters 5, 6, and 7 we discuss how to make the most of your online education investment. You learn how to manage your time, conduct yourself professionally, and avoid plagiarism. Beyond the basics, you understand how to make thoughtful contributions that resonate, submit assignments, and acquire new skills for learning online. Finally, we explain what it takes to be a dynamic, effective, and productive group member.

In Chapters 8 and 9 we show you how to reflect on your own performance and offer constructive feedback to your instructors and your peers. We provide you with guidance on how to be an effective online student going forward.

We conclude with recommendations for keeping in touch with your classmates and faculty in Chapter 9. Finally, we share tips for life-long learning, on site or online.

Introduction

Each chapter concludes with a list of takeaways to apply to your online learning experiences. The examples and tips serve to ground the principles to practices. Finally, all the illustrations focus on the important parts of the "screen," not a specific platform or tool.

The accompanying website (savvyonlinestudent.com) is organized around activities that you can try out in a real online community. In particular, for students we provide:

- a *real online course* with activities for you to practice and interact with other learners world-wide; and

- a set of select *readings* and *resources* relevant to identifying your learning styles, working in virtual teams, and communicating in an online course.

For faculty and those who coordinate online programs, we provide:

- a pre-built *online orientation course* that can be customized for your institution;

- a *PowerPoint presentation* that can be used on site to introduce the online teaching and learning process; and

- a *checklist* for developing and maintaining an online community of learners at your institution.

Chapter 1

Getting a Strong Start Online

As an online student, you will use many of the same skills you have developed in school and life, but you will also build new ones. After reading this chapter, you will understand different course formats, know how to make a positive first impression online, allocate time for your online studies and see how you learn best. At the core, online learning is learning. The key difference? You will be using digital tools instead of analog ones. Instead of going to a physical classroom, you will be learning, communicating, interacting, and participating in digital spaces.

What Are Common Online Course Formats?

There are a few different formats for online courses: at your own pace; live online in real time; or some combination of the two:

At Your Own Pace (also known as asynchronous). You follow a schedule established by your instructor and complete assignments, readings, and participation activities on a regular basis (usually a few times a week). A common misconception is that you are just interacting with materials and working independently. Instead, your instructor will provide you with regular, personalized feedback. You'll also engage in online conversations with your class.

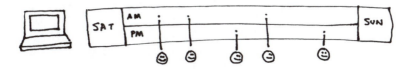

Figure 1.1 Taking an online course at your own pace

Real-Time Online (also known as synchronous). Your teacher and your classmates are all online at the same time. You interact via text, voice, video, or some combination. When signing up for these courses you will know the meeting schedule ahead of time (e.g., Tuesdays and Thursdays at 6:30 p.m.).

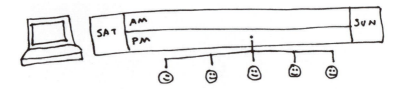

Figure 1.2 Taking an online course with online meetings blended or hybrid

Blended or Hybrid. Some time is spent learning online at your own pace, and some on in-class learning. This means you'll be attending class on site part of the time. The remainder of the class meetings will take place online. This is a popular format for intensive programs, whereby students meet in person once at the beginning, middle and end of a course or program.

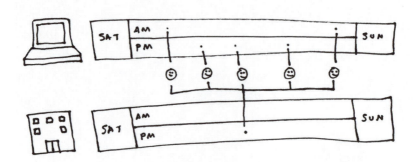

Figure 1.3 Taking a blended course with in-person meetings and online coursework

Preparing Yourself to Study and Engage with Course Materials

Online courses require significant effort on the part of both the professor and the students. One of the most common remarks that we hear from faculty and students alike is: "I am surprised by how much work learning online is . . . I find my online courses are more demanding."

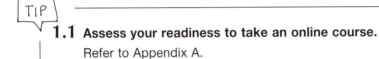

TIP

1.1 Assess your readiness to take an online course.
Refer to Appendix A.

On-site courses set the bar for online courses. Traditionally, accrediting organizations measure classroom time to determine credit hours. A 3-credit course at a U.S. university or college meets for 2 to 3 hours per week over 15 weeks. For every hour spent in class, instructors expect students to spend 2 hours outside class. Over an entire semester, that adds up to a minimum of 45 hours of class time and 90 hours of student preparation time. Online courses use the same numbers but instead of attending classes, students complete assignments—including contributing to online discussions, reflecting on what they know and what they are learning, working collaboratively with peers on projects, and more. Finally, many institutions offer online courses in compressed formats. Instead of meeting over 15 weeks, students complete courses in 5 to 6 weeks. Though the duration may be shorter, the total amount of time your instructors expect you to invest holds constant.

To do well in an online course, you must manage your time effectively. You will need to find new ways to pace yourself, because class goes on throughout the week. Students in face-to-face courses use class meetings as guideposts to help prepare for class. Each meeting functions as an interim deadline, and there are fewer consequences for putting off work. For online courses, expect to spend considerable time every week working on assignments, participating in online conversations, and collaborating on projects with your peers. One way to ensure that you spend enough time on your class is to set up specific times that you login to work.

On site, much of the teaching happens in the interactions that students have with one another and their professors. Unlike an on-site class where students turn in assignments during class, online, students complete multiple assignments and meet interim deadlines all week long. For example, in Ted's Research Methods class, students complete a weekly group research assignment, due on Wednesdays. In addition, they complete a learning journal reflection on Sundays. They do all this work in addition to producing early draft papers, writing a final paper and delivering a final group presentation.

Join Your Online Courses

Figure 1.4 shows how an online class progresses. Before the course officially begins you sign on, meet your professor and peers, and introduce yourself.

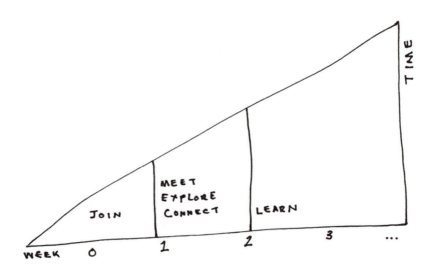

Figure 1.4 Sequence of activities in an online course

At this early phase, we recommend that you review the syllabus, assignments, and readings. This step will help prepare you for the coming weeks, where you will engage in the course readings, discussions, and assignments.

For on-site classes, the work usually begins with the first class session. Online classes work a bit differently. Before class begins, you will receive an email from your institution with your account information, which includes details of where to sign in as well as your username and password. Think of these credentials as your digital identification card. Expect to receive this information about a week before the official start date of the course.

TIP

1.2 Managing lots of passwords. Instead of creating weak passwords or using the same one, use a password manager to keep track of all of your usernames and passwords. Alternatively, maintain a plain text file of passwords, and store it on an external USB drive and store it away from the computer.

Once you have this information, you can sign into your institution's online learning environment—which is often described as a "learning management system," or LMS for short. This LMS portal page contains links to your courses, announcements from your institution, and perhaps an activity stream—news about what people are working on or thinking about (see Figure 1.5 for an example). We recommend signing in as soon as you receive your account details so that you can make sure that your username and password work and that you have access to the correct courses. You'll also have a chance to build your online profile (see Chapter 3 for details).

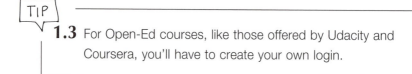

TIP

1.3 For Open-Ed courses, like those offered by Udacity and Coursera, you'll have to create your own login.

Try it!

1.1 Curious what an online course looks like? Create an account at http://savvyonlinestudent.com/tryit and try it. We'll refer back to this site throughout the book.

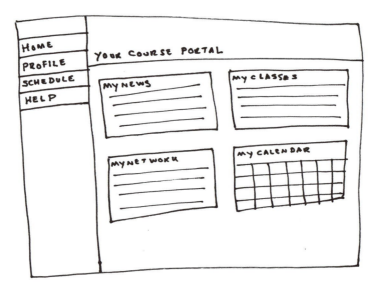

Figure 1.5 The portal page for an LMS

Explore Your Course

Once inside, one of the first things you should see is a welcome announcement from your instructor that highlights the course's learning objectives. You'll also see a link to the course syllabus. Much as with on-site courses, the syllabus provides a roadmap for what's to come. Read the syllabus carefully (see the example on p. 8). It sets out course objectives, assignments, required readings, and meeting times, if any. Use this first visit to note the course goals, what reading materials are required, and when the major assignments are due. Record your assignment deadlines in a calendar. Acquire any required materials, such as textbooks, course packs, or software.

In addition to the syllabus, professors often post other instructional materials, such as exercises, podcasts, lecture notes, and so on. In online courses, like on-site courses, part of your learning will come through reading, listening, or watching prepared materials like books, articles, lectures, or videos. As you look over these materials, estimate how much time you will have to spend studying them.

> **TIP**
>
> **1.4** Understand the course format and learning toolset. Take the time to familiarize yourself with the toolset used in your online course. See if your institution offers any training or an online student orientation. Participate in these sessions to learn about the tools and unique resources that your institution offers. These orientations also provide an opportunity to meet students outside of any classes you are taking—and are something like a digital version of the campus quad. For more on technology, see Chapter 2.

Depending upon how early you visit, the professor may or may not have posted the course materials. If they are not available when you visit, check back at least one week before the start of the course.

Data Visualization Syllabus

Instructor Information: Kristen Sosulski, Clinical Assistant Professor | email@address.com.

Course Format

This is an online course that runs from September 28 to December 10. There are no meeting times.

Course Description

This course is an introduction to the principles and techniques for data visualization. Visualizations are graphical depictions of data that can improve comprehension, communication, and decision making.

Learning Outcomes

- Understand and apply strategies of analytical design;
- identify appropriate data visualization techniques given particular requirements imposed by the data;
- analyze and critique examples of visualizations;
- interpret meaning from multidimensional formats and presentation techniques;
- use techniques learned to generate visualizations.

Course Requirements

Online class participation in discussions	10%
Assignments	50%
Final Project and Online Presentation	40%

Required Reading

Yau, N. (2011). *Visualize This: The Flowing Data Guide to Design, Visualization, and Statistics*. Indianapolis: O'Reilly.

Course Outline / Weekly Schedule

Week 1 Introduction to information visualization.

* Online class discussion: Online discussion of Hans Rosling's Ted Talk: www.ted.com/speakers/hans_rosling.html.

Sample online syllabus

Meeting Your Professor and Peers

Learning is a social process. In addition to gaining new knowledge about the subject you are studying, it is also important to get to know your peers. Introduce yourself. Your contributions—along with those of your professor and peers—make up the learning community. See the example below for how your professor may prompt you to communicate with your fellow classmates.

Dear Students,

Welcome to Research Methods! I am looking forward to getting to know all of you and encourage you to get to know one another.

To get things started, I would like everyone to introduce yourselves. To do so visit the "Forums" section in the course, and create a new topic in the "Introduce Yourself" discussion, "Introducing Your Name."

In your topic, tell us:

(1) why you are taking this class;

(2) what you hope to learn in this course;

(3) how you think this knowledge might be applied in your career;

(4) how you stay abreast of current events and of news in your field;

(5) the last great book you read.

You should also post links to your ePortfolios. I expect every student to have an ePortfolio, with a picture and relevant work samples.

I encourage you to comment on the postings of your classmates, by replying to their posting. I will also post a bit more about myself.

Best,

Professor Marcus

Sample email from an online professor prompting students to introduce themselves

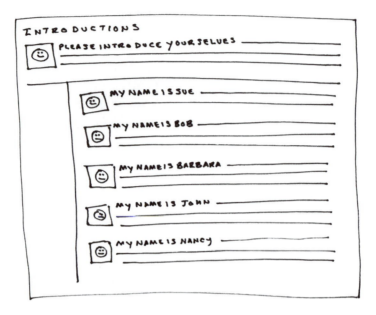

Figure 1.6 A discussion forum with class introductions

Introductions typically take place in a discussion forum. As the saying goes, "First impressions are lasting impressions." Do your best to address the questions your professor asks and start to find things you have in common with your fellow students. Read the introductions of your peers. Visit their online profiles. Identify areas of shared interest. Comment on their introductions. Engage with your professor who may have posted an introduction as well.

Engage in the Learning Process

All of the preceding activities take place before class officially begins. This early start is a unique feature of learning online. When the course starts, what should you expect?

Expect to learn independently. This means that, it's critical for you to follow the course syllabus and know what you are supposed to do and when. Once you have a sense of the deadlines and requirements, start with what's due first. Your learning in the online course is guided by the learning outcomes set by your instructor. These are usually explicit in the course syllabus.

Note the learning outcomes in the example syllabus and our discussion in Chapter 8, p. 89. The learning outcomes speak to the content you'll learn in the course and how you'll learn it. For example, in a data visualization course, you need to apply techniques that you read about and critiqued earlier to generate your own visualization.

How do you learn? If you understand how you learn, you will be a more effective learner, and perhaps more tolerant of those who have a style different from your own. One of the most popular, research-based methods for assessing learning styles is VARK, which reveals your preferences for learning visually, aurally, or kinesthetically, in other words, by seeing, hearing/reading, or by doing. Take a few minutes to determine how you learn best by taking the VARK questionnaire at www.vark-learn.com/english/page.asp?p= questionnaire.

Use your strengths. One you've identified your learning strength, next determine how you learn best. Many materials and resources in an online course are digital. If you notice your class is very "text" heavy and you're a visual learner, you might ask your professor for additional visual resources, or seek them out yourself. See Table 1.1 for best format for digital materials for your learning strength.

In the following chapters, you will learn more about what happens in online courses. Your course may be a self-paced GRE prep course or an open-enrollment/open education course with few stringent requirements. However, whether the course is for credit, self-improvement, free or paid, the more you engage with the course content the more you will learn and the more satisfying your online learning experience will be. Apply takeaways from this chapter to get off to a strong start online.

Table 1.1 Best ways to learn based on your learning strength

Learning Strength	Best Way to Learn	Best Digital Formats
Visual	Seeing and reading	Maps, diagrams, charts, videos, outlines, designs, patterns, shapes
Auditory	Listening and speaking	Lecture, group discussion, audio recordings, online chat, webinars
Read/Write	Information presented as words	Writing/reading essays, reports, lists, diaries, quotations
Kinesthetic	Doing, practical hands-on experiences	Demonstrations, practice, simulations, case studies

Takeaways

— Understand different course formats.

— Assess your readiness to learn online.

— Participate in your institution's online student orientation.

— Get more comfortable with your institution's learning management system (LMS).

— Introduce yourself to your instructor and peers.

— Carefully review the course syllabus.

— Note important course deadlines in your calendar.

— Determine how you learn best.

— Dedicate time to your online studies.

Chapter 2

Your Online Learning Toolkit

May you have 1,000 backups and never need one.
> —David Lerner, the owner of Tekserve, a well-known
> computer retailer, in New York City

When you take on-site courses, you go to a building, find the classroom and take a seat. As a student, the school's expectation is that you bring yourself, and have a way of taking notes—whether it's pen and paper, a laptop, or tablet. Compare this familiar approach to online, where your computing devices and network connection form essential parts of the digital classroom. Though the requirements for online learning are more sophisticated, they are easy to meet. In this chapter we offer advice on getting the right gear for learning online, from making sure you have a modern computer, and a robust internet connection to tips for using collaboration tools and setting up an effective study space.

Should I Buy a New Computer?

You need a computer to access your online class, complete assignments, and join live class meetings or study groups. We've all taken classes in a dingy room with poor light, uncomfortable chairs, and inflexible spaces. Avoid creating the digital equivalent of a bad classroom for yourself. Instead, create a sturdy technical platform to allow you to focus on your studies, instead of being on the phone with technical support.

Savvy Student Principles for Buying a Computer

- Don't let outdated or poor technology tools be a barrier to learning.

- Update your computer every two years.

- Buy as much computer, including storage space and physical memory (RAM), as you can afford.

- Avoid netbooks. A netbook may be fine for when you are on the go, but being a full participant in an online environment may be challenging if it is your online machine.

- Consider buying a laptop, and an external monitor, keyboard, and mouse or trackpad. This makes juggling multiple windows, or comparing documents, easier.

Mac, PC, or Linux?

The debate about which type of computer and operating system to purchase, though still almost religious in nature, is not as important as it once was. The system that you know best is the right system. PCs and Macs are compatible with one another and will play nicely with almost all LMSs. Linux now comes pre-installed on some systems and can be easy to use, but check to make sure that your institution's tools are compatible.

What About Mobile Devices?

You may be wondering, can I just use an iPad, or another smart phone or tablet, for my online class? Our answer: only for some things. A portable electronic device can be handy to listen to a podcast, get notifications, or even compose pithy thoughts on the go. However, you'll need a laptop to do more intensive tasks, such as presenting during a class meeting or editing a video. As of this writing, software for creating and editing documents and for joining web meetings is still evolving on mobile devices.

Think of your mobile devices as part of the ecosystem for learning online. Smart phones enable you to get announcements on the go. You can access course content, whether it's a reading or a podcast, and consume it wherever your are. You could be reading the reflections of your colleagues or thinking about how to respond to a discussion post. You could even compose responses on your smart phone or tablet.

However, the absence of a physical keyboard can also limit your participation. Dictation software is still evolving. These limitations mean that you should think of your smart phone or tablet as a supporting but not a main player in your online learning experience. Use it to stay connected, for study, and for quick participation. Your laptop or desktop is where you do the bulk of your studying.

eReaders

eReaders, whether Kindles, iPads, or other tablets, have become more popular options for distributing course reading materials. Instead of having to pick up a paper course pack from the bookstore, you order digital copies of course reading materials in electronic format and download them to your eReader. Companies like Xanedu provide eBooks. New textbook publishers, like Inkling, make books designed for tablets that include enhanced features such as videos, scored quizzes, social bookmarking, and note taking. Depending upon your course format, you may be able to access your reading materials on a range of devices. Explore tablet programs for highlighting, note taking and collaborative capabilities. They can make it easier than printing and marking up paper documents.

Web Meetings

You may join a web conference at some point with your classmates, or your online class may have set online meeting dates and times. These are online meetings that take place in real time, where you can see and hear one another via your webcam. You may be tempted to go to an internet cafe or coffee shop to do your work. This approach can be fine for working on an assignment, but it will prevent you from being an effective participant in a web meeting. There is just too much ambient noise. Also, your classmates and instructor are likely to find background changes, such as people walking back and forth behind you, distracting.

See p. 36 in Chapter 4 to learn how to run a successful online meeting. Also, see Chapter 5 for some ways in which web meetings can be used in your online class.

Be Aware of What Falls in Your Camera's View

You might not want to show off your collection of vintage teddy bears, your child's toys or your unboxed Star Wars action figures. Call us old fashioned, but we don't like it when students participate in synchronous classes while seated on a couch or in bed (yes, this happens, and we notice.) Participating from these spaces gives the impression that you are not taking your learning seriously. Instead, consider a more traditional setup, such as a table or desk with a comfortable chair.

Pay attention to your webcam's angle. Web cameras are often integrated into your laptop or desktop, which can make moving them challenging. Still, make an effort to position the camera so that it is at or near eye level. Laptops benefit from being raised a few inches on a stand. Desktop monitors can be adjusted or tilted to a flattering angle.

Be Aware of Your Room's Lighting

Much of how you appear on camera has to do with lighting. A good source of natural light coming from the side is best. Still, your meetings may not occur during daylight hours or in a place where there is a window. Overhead sources generate shadows that are not flattering. Low light makes for a grainy picture. The light your computer emits is not sufficient and is unflattering. If natural light is not an option, then gentle, indirect light sources, such as an incandescent lamp with a neutral shade, provide a more flattering picture.

Helpful Tools and Tips for Good Sound and Web Meetings

Participating in live meetings is more technically complex than visiting web pages. Having the right gear and mindset can help you avoid problems, or offer alternatives if the primary tool fails. See Figure 2.1 for the essentials for a great web meeting:

- Having a speakerphone or even a smart phone with a speakerphone that gets good reception is a valuable backup if things go awry.

- If you are using a mobile phone, connect it to a power source.

- If you do have to call into a live session, or conference call, be sure to mute your phone when you are not speaking. Open microphones add unwanted background noise.

Figure 2.1 Good room setup for web meetings

- Earbuds or headsets reduce or eliminate the dreaded echo that is all too common in group video conference sessions.

Backup Your Data and Test Your Backup

A Few Comments From Ted on Backups . . .

I have not suffered a catastrophic loss of data, but have come close twice—these near death data experiences have forced me to focus on having a reliable backup plan. Here is how mine works for my home office:

Time Machine backup for my iMac. I have an external drive, which I "set and forget" to back up automatically. This way, if I lose a file, or even want to go back to an earlier version of one, I just launch Time Machine and I can travel back to get the file I want.

Entire, bootable version of my iMac. Every week, a script copies the entire contents of my Mac onto an external drive. I could connect this drive to any other Mac and boot into it—so my applications as well as my data are preserved. This backup would be useful in the event the hard drive on the Mac failed.

Hosted, off-site backup. All data files, including all pictures, and music are backed up to a third-party hosted service. This scenario is pretty grim. Something terrible would have to happen to my home office, but it also has other benefits—all of my files are "in the cloud" and accessible from wherever I may be.

Perhaps you know the sinking feeling that comes with having lost a computer, or hard drive with family photos or videos along with thousands of other files that you have long since forgotten about. Losing data is a common occurrence. Hardware fails. We might make a mistake and accidentally delete a file, an entire folder or even a hard drive. The good news is that it's never been easier to back up your data. Here are three key steps:

1. Have a plan for your backup. A good practice is to keep one backup at your home, and another off-site. This way, if something happens at home, your data will be safe elsewhere.

2. Implement your plan. Backups only work if they are running. A good approach is to set your backup to run at regular intervals, say every day at midnight.

3. Test your recovery options. Pretend you lost a file or set of files. Attempt to recover them from your backup.

What About the Cloud? What is the Cloud?

No, we are not talking about beautiful forms of water vapor in the sky above. We are talking about how easy it is to store your data on a third-party server and have it available at any time. There are many services, from DropBox to Google Drive. We use them and recommend them. Even so, consider that those services can have outages, or change their terms of service, which could render your data inaccessible. We recommend that you maintain your own copies of files, emails and photos stored with third-party vendors. By having redundant data, you reduce your risk of losing an important assignment.

Preparing for Online Collaboration

We have dedicated an entire chapter to group projects, which you will encounter during your online learning experience, but we want to devote some time to tools and strategies for effective online collaboration.

Consider the following assignment:

Each week, your group will identify between 10 and 15 articles from academic journals that are relevant to your group's topic. Post a brief summary of the article, and how it relates to your group's topic to the class discussion forum.

If you were working with five other team members, how would you approach this assignment to produce a single document with these references?

One way would be to appoint a collector, and everyone could email their summaries to him. The collector would post them all to a document for the group to review.

A better way would be to create a document that everyone can edit. That way, each group member would post their contributions directly to the document. Google Docs or Microsoft Office 365 support this kind of collaboration.

There are many tools to help groups work together online, and they are always changing. Your school's LMS may have dedicated collaboration spaces, such as workgroups for in-class collaboration. In our classes, we make a point of creating study group spaces for students. This way, as instructors, we have a window into our students' work process as well as the final product. Review the course syllabus and any posted materials to learn what your instructor has to say about how electronic collaboration. If guidelines are specified, follow them. If they are not, consider the goals of the project—what are the interim deliverables? What is the final product? How will the tool or tools support the development of the final product? Choose the best tools to support the project goals. Collaboration tools are changing how we work. Table 2.1 illustrates two approaches to working together. Consider these as you develop a process for working with your team.

Regardless of which tool or tools you chose, be sure that you all are on the same page. Make sure that everyone can access the tools and has a basic understanding of how to use them.

Keep One Another Up to Date

Many modern collaboration tools will keep track of the contributions that you make to a document, tracking things like total editing time, and who made what changes. Bear in mind that this data is also

Table 2.1 Two approaches to online collaboration

The Old Way	The New Way
• Email—send documents back and forth.	• Collaborate on documents "in the cloud," using a service like Office Live, Google Docs, or Dropbox.
Pros	
• Method is well understood and widely used. • Tools are available on people's desktops—no new accounts required. • Robust editing and text formatting features. • It just works. • Many people may edit simultaneously. • Work process and product are more transparent.	• Versions managed by software. • Many people may edit simultaneously. • Work process and product are more transparent.
Cons	
• Only one person can be editing the document at a time. • Many versions of a single document get created and it's not clear which version is the definitive one. • Production takes more time because the document is passed from person to person. • Work process is not transparent. • It is more difficult for the instructor to provide feedback to group. • Yet another account to manage.	• Some team members may have to learn new tools. • Yet another account to manage.

available to your professors when evaluating assignments. Still, it's a good idea to keep all team members up to date about your contributions to an assignment. There are many different ways to keep your team members in the loop. You might keep a running list of important changes (e.g., "added new section on collaboration— Ted B") at the beginning of the document.

You could also send an email to your teammates, or post about your activity in the LMS' workgroup, or another shared space. Using these tools helps build cohesion among your team and generates momentum for your project.

What If I'm On the Road or Away From Home?

One of the advantages of learning online is that you can participate from almost anywhere—or at least any place that has a reliable internet connection. Also, time differences can be significant, depending upon how far you are from your school's home base so plan to maximize your contributions so that your contributions mesh well with your classmates' or teammates'. If you are planning on leading or participating in a presentation while away, then reach out to the venue where you will be staying and see if there is a reliable internet connection. Hotel wifi, though ubiquitous and free, can be unreliable. Make an advance plan of how you will participate from the road in case things go awry.

Getting Help When You Need It

The best time to get help is before a technical problem becomes a crisis. Try things out in advance. We allow and encourage students to access courses well in advance of the official start date of the class. Sign into your course as soon as possible. Check to see if your institution offers "live" office hours. This offers students not only a chance to their classes but to practice using the synchronous classroom with other students and an instructor. It's human nature to procrastinate and think that you'll just work things out before your first class, but that's usually not enough time. Before you take an on-site course, you peruse the syllabus. You come to class prepared to take notes. Saying that you have a technical problem during your first online class is akin to pulling the emergency brake on a crowded subway if you're not feeling well: you are asking the instructor to stop, and everyone to wait, so that you can resolve your issue. Instead, make a positive impression on your peers. Arrive early, and try out the environment beforehand. You will impress your peers and your instructor.

Just as things sometimes get in our way in an on-site classroom— markers or a whiteboard eraser go missing—things may go wrong online: for example, a plug-in refuses to load to a browser not rendering a page correctly. When this happens, visit the troubleshooting tips in the Appendix B.

One of the challenging things about taking online classes is that the technology is always changing. So even if things work well one day, they might not work well the next. Malicious hackers write programs to infect computers. Vendors like Apple and Microsoft regularly release updates to address security holes found by hackers or to fix things that are wrong. Chances are that your school's software providers are doing the same thing. Factor in all of these changes and the dependency of your own technology and you have got a potential recipe for frustration. Being prepared, and having a resilient mindset, will help you overcome these problems and thrive online.
Don't let your computer or your lack of preparation kill your online learning experience.

Takeaways

Review this list to ensure you have all the components of your online learning toolkit. Have you:

— Purchased computer in the last two years.

— Installed the latest operating system, updates, and web browsers.

— Tested your webcam.

— Confirmed that lighting and camera angle are good.

— Bought headset/headphones available for a backup.

— Invested in a high quality chair for web meetings and your online work in general.

— Set up in an uncluttered place for video conferences.

— Got a backup communication device handy.

— Made sure your computer's backup is set, running, and tested.

— Explored new collaboration tools.

Chapter 3

The Digital You

When you study online, you learn about your classmates and your professor through the digital information they present about themselves. In this chapter, we'll provide ways for you to form your digital presence in the online classroom.

We all have digital identities. Some of you may even have multiple online profiles, telling a different story about yourself depending upon the audience. These profiles make up a unique digital footprint. Most universities and colleges have a social networking platform to enable you to create a digital profile or portfolio. Doing so is an important first step in forming your academic digital presence.

Figure 3.1 Online student profile page

How would you like to be perceived by your peers and professors? Having a thoughtful answer to this question will help you build a strong online profile and credible reputation. In an online classroom, the digital identity you create and maintain defines you. An accurate portrait helps your professors and other students learn more about you, your interests and your experience. Good professors avail themselves of this knowledge about their students to tailor instruction. You'll also forge stronger bonds with your peers if you are more than just a name on a screen.

Building Your Online Academic Profile

When you register for an online course, you may receive an email to login to your course. Upon login, you may be asked to provide some information about yourself to form your initial online student digital profile. These academic profiles are similar to those you might create on Facebook or LinkedIn, but unlike those sites, these pages showcase your academic interests, even if you are still discovering what those interests are. What do you notice about the sample profile in Figure 3.1? Your profile will most likely begin as a space in which you present some of your academic, professional, and personal interests to the online learning community. Update your profile as you go, and as your studies continue; this will develop into a rich ePortfolio in which you display and share your work. Strong ePortfolios are more than spaces for collecting and sharing your work. The best students use them to reflect upon their accomplishments. See Figure 3.2 for an example of accomplishments listed in an ePortfolio.

Begin your academic digital identity by logging in and accessing your institution's LMS. If you don't know how to do that, contact your school's help desk. Find where to post information such as a photo, bio, résumé, and your accomplishments:

Post a photo. To begin, post a professional looking picture of yourself. While your profile picture should reflect your personality, it also should be a picture that is appropriate for an academic or business settings. Good pictures let people put a face with your name. Try and choose one where you are the only subject in the photo. Avoid using a group photo and then cropping out everyone but yourself. The result is less than professional (see Figure 3.3). Consider having a friend who is skilled with a camera take your picture. Photos of you in a professional setting, such as making a presentation, can also work well.

Figure 3.2 Accomplishments in a student portfolio

Figure 3.3 Good versus poor online profile pictures

An online student biography

I'm a senior at the University of American Colleges studying economics and poverty. My senior thesis compares the poverty levels of today's Americans compared to thirty years ago.

For the past three years, I've been an intern for the Federal Reserve Bank of New York.

Write your bio. A biography should include brief information about your professional work experience, internships, academic experience, and achievements. Refer to the biography above for an example. Write in a professional tone. Using the first person feels more approachable for online courses. Your most recent credential should go first. Since your biography is a digital document, link to projects and websites that reflect your accomplishments. Your classmates may reference your biography to learn more about who's who in their class.

Share your résumé. Your résumé is a detailed summary of your work experience, awards, skills, academic experience, publications, and relevant projects. Share your skills, including technical knowledge, languages spoken, and any awards you have received. Keep your résumé up to date and link it to your ePortfolio or profile. For details on how to create a compelling résumé contact your institution's career services office. They should be able to advise you.

Purdue's Online Writing Lab also has excellent tips on developing a professional résumé: http://owl.english.purdue.edu/owl/resource/719/01/.

> **TIP**
>
> **3.1** **Use a consistent link for your résumé.** One way to accomplish this would be to save your résumé to a site like Scribd or Google Docs that way, you have a single consistent link and embeddable file. Also, when you update your résumé, you can simply "upload a new version," rather than creating copy. The link always goes to the most recent document.

Sample student résumé

Sonny Mukherjee
sonny@email.com | (917) 222-0990
http://sonnym.com

EDUCATION
Bachelor of Science, **Expected 2015**
New York University, Stern School of Business, New York
Major: Marketing and Journalism

WORK EXPERIENCE

Intern, CBS News
September 2012–Present

* Researched news articles related to current events
* Collaborated with journalists for lead generation

Intern, Pepsi Co.
September 2011–December 2012

* Managed social media presence for two PepsiCo brands
* Used Facebook and Twitter to launch digital marketing campaigns

COMPUTER SKILLS
Proficient in SAS, R, Microsoft Office

LANGUAGES
Fluent in English, French, and Hindi

Maintaining a Positive Digital Identity

Given how easy it is to find out information about people via the web, it's important to cultivate a positive online identity. Typing a name into a web browser search box yields hundreds of results, from the sorts of digital profiles we discussed, to posts on social networks like Twitter, Facebook, or Google Plus, or third-party websites that index and resell personal information. Chances are that you are on more than one social network. Your Facebook friends probably differ from your LinkedIn connections. What you post on a school profile focuses on academic accomplishments. Keep your different audiences in mind, and beware that they can overlap in unexpected ways. What if a professional connection is also a Facebook friend, and she sees pictures in your activity stream from a party that got out of hand? Remember, search engines like Google and Bing index and store your digital footprint. The more you do online, the more visible you are. Once something is posted on a public website, it is difficult to hide or erase. Be thoughtful about what you post. Privacy controls offer a false sense of security. Bad posts can come back to haunt you later.

TIP
3.2 Learn more about your professor. See if you can learn more about your professor by searching Google or reviewing his/her digital profile on your institution's web site or by going to http://ratemyprofessor.com.

Use the Right Tone and Tools

Your communication, writing style, and your digital profile comprise the digital you.

Consider the tone of your writing. When connecting with peers, use a friendly, more casual tone. When communicating with your professor, be polite and write in a more formal tone and style.

When writing emails, use greetings and salutations. Always address the person to whom you are writing by name. Sign your emails. Email is the best way to communicate with your professor about questions that are specific to your academic progress in the course. These types of questions are inappropriate to post publicly in the online course, for example on a discussion forum. Try to avoid asking your professor questions that can be answered by reading the syllabus. Also, be sure you are polite and respectful when asking questions of your professor and peers. The examples below illustrate an appropriate email to your professor, compared with an inappropriate message.

Example of inappropriate and appropriate emails to your professor

Inappropriate	**Appropriate**
Hi.	Dear Professor,
Can you please tell me what I'm supposed to do this week in the course? I am really confused and need a response ASAP!	I am a little unclear about the activities that are due this week. Would you mind clarifying when assignment 1 is due and where I should submit it? Thank you.
– Tom	Best Regards,
	Tom

The Importance of Presence

Presence in an online class is more about keeping your profile up to date. It's about regularly connecting with your professor and classmates. As Brandi Scollins-Mantha explains, social presence requires "more than just being with another, but being connected or engaged in some form of exchange." There are several measures of presence that your professor can track. These include how often you login, how much time you spend in each section of the course

Table 3.1 Calculated course metrics and student activity

Metric	Measurement
Most recent login	Date and time
Cumulative time spent in course	Hours, minutes, seconds
Most recently viewed items	List of course materials "clicked" on
Number of discussion forum posts	Number discussion forum topics posted
Assignments submission status	A list of complete and incomplete assignments by student
Grades by assignment, quiz, exam, and participation	Automated grading of multiple choice, fill-in the blank, matching question type tests and/or quizzes

(i.e. syllabus, lessons, forums, resources, modules) and in-course as an aggregate (see Table 3.1). Universities use this data to see how you are doing and measure academic performance.

Your presence should be palpable, and you should be aware of the virtual presence of your peers and instructor. Here are some different ways to be present in an online course:

Logging in. Your professor knows how much time you've spent logged into the online course and what pages you've visited. Some LMSs provide footprints on the first page of the site to show the most recent visitors. You should login regularly, at least 3 to 4 times per week, and plan on making contributions to the classroom community while there.

Participating in online discussions. Contributing to ongoing conversations is key to demonstrating your active presence in the online course. These conversations happen in public for all class members to observe and contribute to.

Assignment completion. Be sure to do the assigned work. Follow instructions. Ask for clarification if need be, before the assignment deadline.

Pose questions. **Offer constructive feedback**. Ask your professor if something is unclear, or if you need more detail to understand a concept. Answers to questions benefit you, but may also benefit your peers. In a similar vein, if something particularly has helped or hindered your learning, let your instructor know. Details on how to offer effective feedback appear in p. 99 Chapter 9, Beyond Your Online Course.

Grading and assessment. Make sure you keep track of how you are being graded and assessed. Review the online grade book in your course and make sure that you are making the progress you expect.

As tools for online learning evolve, more real-time data become available concerning your interactions and performance. However, it's the meaningful *qualitative contributions*—keeping up with work—that matters most. Tracking is not learning. Your professor will use the metrics that matter most to achieve the course objectives.

Takeaways

By now you should have the confidence to create an appropriate digital profile and portfolio. You should have a sense of how best to communicate in the digital space, and how to continue to evaluate and evolve your digital identity. Review this list of takeaways to guide the development of the digital you:

— Post a professional photograph of yourself.

— Write and post a biography.

— Add your résumé.

— Link to relevant projects and websites on your profile.

— Make regular updates to your digital profile.

— Login to the course regularly, at least three times per week.

— Contribute to the online course conversations.

Chapter 4

Getting to Know Your Faculty and Peers

Learning is social. Get to know the people in your course. Your professor, teaching assistants, and fellow students will help you understand concepts and serve as sounding boards for your ideas. This chapter will (1) help you understand different online communication channels; (2) ensure you know how to join online conversations; and (3) show you how to engage with your classmates. In time and with practice, having conversations online will feel like second nature.

Communication Modes

Communication takes different forms in online courses; to be successful, you need to understand these communication modes and channels. Communication modes include written, visual, recorded audio/video, and live audio/video formats. Just as in the physical world, different digital spaces lend themselves to different kinds of communication. You would not schedule an important conversation with your boss or doctor outside on a noisy city street. Online, it would be poor form to cut and paste a six-page essay into a discussion forum—that approach would be equivalent to offering an hour-long, uninterrupted lecture over dinner. While it is possible to use both of these approaches to get your message across, you will have a better chance of being heard if you choose the right venue and form. Consider these online communication modes (see Figure 4.1):

> **Writing**. Online courses require lots of writing. You can write to your classmates and professor in the discussion forums, in a live text chat, in blogs, wikis, shared web-based documents, social networks, instant messages, and

Figure 4.1 Online course communication modes

How to Record a Short Video or Audio Clip

Sidebar 4.1

Most computers, tablets and smart phones make it easy to make a video or audio recording. Here are some general tips on making a good video or audio recording:

1. Have some sense of what you're going to say before you press record. You don't need a script, but you do need a few concrete ideas.

2. Understand how the tool you are using works. Do a test recording or two to make sure that you know how to stop and start. Play the recording back to make sure that it's clear.

3. Address the person directly—don't be too formal, e.g., "Chip, I like what you did with the introduction—it really captured my attention but I wasn't clear what you were talking about in the second paragraph—I got lost on Thermodynamics."

so on. If your class setup has a live chat, learn when your classmates and professor will be online. When writing messages in a discussion forum, tell the system to notify you when there are new posts, or check back often. While there, read new posts and add to the discussion.

Sharing. Share your ideas and relevant resources. To better convey your message, share resources—from articles you find online, to new research from the field, to video broadcasts. Social networks like Facebook, Twitter and Google Plus make sharing easy. For example, Facebook's wall allows you and your friends to post video, images, polls, in addition to text. On social networks, most people respond better to multimedia than to text or polls. Your institution's LMS may have a similar feature set: if so, make good use of it. If not, then consider creating a group for your class to share media on a social networking site.

Recording. Record audio and/or video. Sometimes it's easier to say to something than to write it. Consider recording brief audio/video clips and share those with your classmates.

Meeting. Host an online meeting with your classmates via live audio and/or video (or even the phone). When brainstorming or trying to make a decision, real-time communication is helpful. If time zones are not an overwhelming obstacle, you can meet live online via Skype or other real-time meeting tools, like Google Hangouts. They're similar to conference calls, but in addition to hearing each other, you can see one another, share documents and chat. Live online meetings (and face-to-face meetings) require some advance planning. For a successful meeting, follow these simple steps:

1. Schedule the meeting in advance.

2. Circulate an agenda for the meeting. If you have many items, allocate time to each item. Make sure to do the high priority items first.

3. Have a facilitator—this person will run the meeting.

4. Have a scribe—this person will record what the group decided, what the action items are, and who's responsible for which item. The scribe should send out the notes of the meeting shortly after the meeting adjourns.

Refer to Chapter 2 (p. 13) and Chapter 5 (p. 43) for more on web meetings.

Seek to Understand and Be Understood

As Palloff and Pratt explained, the goal of any online interaction is to be "properly understood" and to "get your points across effectively." When taking an online course, all of your communication will be mediated through some communications tool. When communicating face-to-face, we have other methods in addition to the message's content to help understand a person, such as non-verbal language and tone. When online, if tools are not video based, those additional feedback channels are lost. Therefore, be aware of how your message is likely to be received and adjust according to the medium.

For text-based communications, such as discussion forums or email, ensure that your tone is conversational and that your messages inspire dialogue. Though email has been part of the online communications tool kit since the 1980s and helped bring the internet into being, scholarly research shows that we often misunderstand one another in email. Kruger, Epley, Parker, and Ng found that "people tend to believe that they can communicate over e-mail more effectively than they actually can." In other words, it is difficult for us to step outside our own perspective and accurately predict how others will interpret our written electronic communications. Once you are aware of these limitations, you can take steps to overcome them.

If no one is responding to your messages, review those postings that have not attracted responses. Reflect on how you can improve your posts to promote more interactions. If you are stumped, ask a friend to take a look at the post to help you understand why others might not be responding or to give you another perspective on your tone. Also consider the time of day that you are posting. If you post late in the evening or the next day, the discussion may already be over:

> **Re-read and spellcheck your work.** Be aware that when communicating in writing, words bear the full weight of your meaning; your audience cannot see your facial expressions, read your body language, or hear your tone. In some cases, it might be helpful to read a message aloud before sending it. Just hearing yourself offers a clue to the tone. Revise your written text if you find that it is out of sync with your intended meaning. Finally, avoid writing long postings on your smartphone to avoid typos or auto-text errors.
>
> Text chats occur in real time, which leads to a more dynamic conversation. However, since you're responding in real time, it is more difficult to spell check your work. Still, we recommend enabling your browser's "check spelling as you type" feature. Here are some expressions that may help during a classroom chat:

DD	due diligence
EM	excuse me
GA	go ahead
GI	google it
GJ	good job
IMCO	in my considered opinion
IME	in my experience
MO	move on
OT	off topic
POV	point of view
SME	subject matter expert
THX	thank you
W/O	without
W/	with

This is a very short list. Check with your instructor and see if abbreviations are appropriate for the discussion, or if your class has an agreed upon chat vocabulary. If your class is chatting regularly, it may be helpful to come up with a shorthand that serves the discussion.

Refer back to Chapter 2 where we discuss how to participate and collaborate effectively using web meeting tools.

Follow the session protocol for contributing to the conversation. The bigger a group is, the more structure is required. In a small group, it is OK to break into the conversation when there is a pause, and you have something to add. In larger group sessions, a moderator might call on folks to keep things moving. Speak clearly and slowly so that you are heard. Listen carefully to your peers. Indicate that you are listening by restating key points of the discussion and connecting them to your contribution.

Employing these tips will help ensure that you are an effective contributor to conversations.

Contributing to the Conversation

There are several ways you can contribute to the class dialogue:

- regularly respond to discussion forum postings with thoughtful comments that are relevant to the person who posted the message;

- for team projects that require intense collaboration or decision making, arrange a live online meeting with a few of your classmates; or

- arrange a chat session with your professor or peers on a recent class reading or article.

The tone and nature of your contributions (in whatever form) should inspire conversation. Ask questions of others. Favor open-ended questions over closed-ended ones. Open-ended questions keep the conversation going.

Closed- and Open-Ended Conversations

Closed-ended:

Name a band that made a significant contribution to rock and roll in the early 21st century.

Open-ended:

What band made significant contributions to rock and roll in the early 21st century? Why? Explain.

Building an Effective Relationship with Your Professor

How do you build an effective relationship with your professor? When pondering this question, it helps to understand that she plays many roles in an online course. She designs the curriculum, manages the online classroom, and assesses your learning. The best way to build an effective relationship is to demonstrate sincere interest in the subject, take the assignments seriously and immerse yourself in the activities she has designed for the course. Ask good questions that help the professor spot an area that's ambiguous. This way, she can provide clarity not only for you, but also for your peers. Be active in the conversations your professor organizes. These online tools facilitate interactions with your professor and peers:

> **Discussion forums**. Discussion forums are a place to introduce yourself to one another, organized around student questions and topics selected by the instructor. This structures the conversation along specific areas of interest for class participants. Typically, there will be a forum dedicated to questions and answers (Q&A).

Online office hours. Usually, you'll find your professor's office hours listed in the syllabus. If you are near your school, you may be able to meet with your professor face-to-face. If not, check to see how you can schedule a meeting with your professor. More often than not, your professor will be open to speaking with you on the phone, via text chat, Skype, or other real-time channels.

Email. You should have your professor's email address from either the syllabus or course site. Though you should not hesitate to contact your professor via email, try to reserve email for answers to questions that are unique to you, as opposed to ones that may benefit the entire class.

Connecting and Networking with Your Peers

Even though you may not meet your classmates in person, there are many ways to connect with one another:

Seek out those with similar interests, experience, or friends. By reviewing the introductions and profiles of your classmates, you may find others who have worked for the same company, for example.

Organize study sessions. A great way to build friendships and partnerships online is to gather together around a common goal, such as studying together for an exam. Tools like OpenStudy.org or Google Hangouts could work well for study sessions.

Connect using social networks. Social networks are great places to build online connections that enhance your online learning experience. Search Facebook or LinkedIn to see if your school has an online presence. Join the networks and see what people are talking about, and if the conversations interest you. You might create a group around your class. OpenStudy also has groups around classes and subjects.

Join student clubs and organizations. Your academic advisor can direct you to some clubs and student organizations that you may be interested in joining. While this is not directly relevant to your coursework, these opportunities for connecting with your school's learning community at large can allow you to feel a part of your institution.

Building and Maintaining Relationships

For some, it's difficult to imagine having a relationship with a person you've never met face to face. A great way to learn more about your classmates is to have a live conversation with them:

Chat sessions and online meet ups. Using simple tools you can host an online text or video chat with your classmates. Good use of these formats facilitates effective and efficient group projects (see Chapter 8).

Coffee houses. If some of your classmates live nearby, consider organizing a meet up at your local coffee house.

Institution sponsored events. Check with student services: your institution may offer gatherings or events that are a good fit for online and on-site students. These events can be a good opportunity to meet your online peers and faculty.

Takeaways

— Seek to understand and be understood.

— Online communication is mediated through tools.

— Communicate effectively by maintaining an awareness of the medium's strengths and weaknesses.

— Make timely, relevant and thoughtful contributions to the course dialogue.

— Build strong relationships with faculty and peers by learning about them and their interests. Share your passions.

Chapter 5

Participating in Your Online Course

In this chapter, we'll discuss how online participation differs from in-class participation. We'll show you how it works, where it takes place, and finally present some tips for making thoughtful contributions.

What is Online Class Participation?

In on-site classes, participation means raising your hand, speaking up, asking questions, offering answers, participating in discussions and more. Participation is more impromptu on site than in an online course. Participating in an online class involves interacting with your professor and peers in digital spaces during structured time periods. Without classroom hours, you could feel a little disconnected from your school, class, instructor, and peers. The absence of body language, eye contact, and physical presence may leave you feeling somewhat disconnected. However, by actively contributing to online conversations and engaging in course activities you gain a sense of connectedness. You will be rewarded with interactions, comments, and feedback for the duration of the course, and friendships that go beyond it.

When exploring your online course (see Chapter 1), note those areas that require your participation. You can easily look at the course navigation for interactive spaces, such as *discussion forums* (see Figure 5.1). These may include video lectures, blogs, discussion forums, or meet ups.

One tactic for succeeding in online classes is establishing a pattern or schedule of participation. Your class may not always meet at the

Figure 5.1 Online course website navigation

same time. Make a commitment to yourself to sign into your course and contribute on specific dates and times. Put these appointments in your calendar and honor them. If you meet these interim steps, the overall workload of the course will be much more manageable than if you have to play catch-up on assignments to meet course deadlines.

> TIP
>
> **5.1** Review the syllabus for your online course and note specific class participation requirements, such as contributions to online discussions.

What Does Active Online Class Participation Look Like?

Much like an on-site class where participation involves more than attending class, online participation involves more than logging in. Think of class participation as an occasion to make contributions to the larger class dialogue. Online class participation takes on many forms, from contributing to a discussion and sharing reflections on your learning to collaborating on a shared text. Responding to questions during a web conference, or working on a group project with your team, are also elements of class participation.

Regardless of the form of the class participation, your contributions take place in digital spaces. Table 5.1 lists the common ways students participate in online courses. You'll notice you can use many of the same technologies for different purposes. If you are unfamiliar with any of the technologies mentioned, simply google them or refer to the glossary at: https://sph.uth.edu/faculty/instructional-development/online-education-glossary/.

Table 5.1 Forms of participation in an online course

Ways You Can Participate	With Whom	Where
Discuss	Large or small group discussion	Discussion boards or forums Blogs Chat rooms
Blog and comment	Shared with class or team	Blogs, Google Docs, Microsoft Word, wikis, discussion boards.
Collaborate with others	Working in a team or pairs	Wikis, Google Docs
Meet online	In a team or large class	Skype, Adobe Connect, WebX, Cisco Telepresence, Google Hangouts
Present via video	An individual or team to the full class	Same as above: PowerPoint, Skype, video conferencing screencast software, live or recorded video

Discussing

A discussion in an online course consists of a topical conversation centered around course content. Typically, your professor will pose a question or prompt, to which the class will respond. These discussions typically take place in a discussion forum (also known as the online bulletin board). However, these discussions could easily take place in a chat room, video conference, or blog. Discussion forums are perhaps the most well known tool—and often what people think about when they think about learning online.

Students will respond to the instructor's prompt, and then to one another. See the example of a prompt below:

Example Prompt

Who won the 1960 Kennedy-Nixon presidential debate? What evidence can you offer in support of your position?

The instructor weighs in at different points to inflect the discussion and keep it on track. When responding to a prompt, address the question or questions the instructor poses. Review the responses of your peers. Think critically. What can you add that has not already been contributed to the discussion? Can you take things in a different direction, or perhaps offer a point of view different from your own? Generally, offer reasons for the position you're taking, and bolster those reasons with evidence from relevant and authoritative sources:

Approaches for Online Discussion. Consider these different methods for joining the fray:

- Agreement—Discuss your level of agreement or disagreement with your classmate's comment and explain why.

- Critique—Provide thoughtful and constructive criticism in response to a classmate's comment.

- Expansion—Elaborate on the ideas or concepts presented by your classmates.

- Examples—Provide examples to illustrate your points or your classmate's comments.

A Note on Politeness

"Keyboard bravery" is a phenomenon where people write things in a discussion forum that they might not say if they were seated next to a person. Unlike a comment in class that could be tempered with an expression or tone, your written words have to carry the entire weight of your meaning. Depending upon the tool that you are using, your words also could have a long shelf life. If you are posting something that feels like it could be controversial, read your post aloud before sharing it. Once it is online, you may not be able to tone it down. (Some systems let you edit after a post; others do not to preserve the integrity of the discussion.) Remember, your peers may know you entirely through your written words and will form an impression of you based on your interactions in these forums.

Sidebar 5.1

In discussions, students can also take on the role of moderator to facilitate the conversation. An instructor may even assign this role to an individual or group. Having the mindset that every participant is responsible for the overall discussion will help the entire class have a richer online experience.

Finally, discussions need not be text based; technologies like VoiceThread allow you to add video comments and have discussions around images or videos. For more, visit: http://voicethread.com/features.

> **TIP**
>
> ## 5.2 Discussion Forum Ground Rules
>
> - Use a friendly tone when conversing with your peers.
> - Be thoughtful. Search before you post to ensure you're not repeating someone else's post.
> - Understand how discussion forums work. Use the *reply* button to comment on a post, rather than posting a new idea.

Examples of online discussions. The "introduce yourself" forum (see Chapter 1, p. 10) is an example of using forums for a social purpose. Topic-driven forums (see Figure 5.2), should mirror a discussion. Typically, the discussion is tied to the grade for the topic-driven forum. Figure 5.2 illustrates an online conversation. The student, Jack, is responding to an assignment with input from others. Notice the application of the *expansion* and

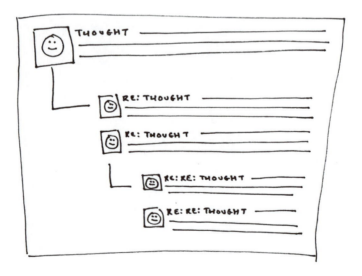

Figure 5.2 Online conversation in an discussion forum

agreement approaches in this conversation. Online conversations of this sort take place over a few days or a few weeks.

Try it!

5.1 Go to our website and select "Discussions" to try it out. Respond to one of the topics posted. Then, leave a comment on someone else's post.

Blogging and Commenting

The word "blog" is a shortened form of "web log," an online tool that makes it easy to publish content, and then have others comment on it. Many online courses incorporate blogging as a course activity. A blog usually has a single author, and is a conversation between the reader and her audience.

When blogs are used in an online course, your content has a prominent place. Instead of writing just for the instructor, students are writing for one another. Typically, in addition to posting content, students can also comment on the work of their peers. See Figure 5.3 for an illustration. Because of their openness and accessibility, blogs help build community and maintain a sense of connection in online classes:

> **Writing an effective blog post**. An effective blog post addresses the topic, or brings in a topic that is relevant to the class, provides specific evidence to support the point you're trying to make, integrates readings from the class, and makes connections to other knowledge areas. Your instructor may have different requirements but generally, blog posts are less formal than papers. It is OK to write in the first person, e.g., "I think that . . ." It is also good

Figure 5.3 A blog posting with student comments

practice to recognize if you are referring to content from another source. Usually, your instructor will have a preferred method (MLA, APA, Chicago, etc.). Your posts will be more authoritative and respected by your peers and colleagues if you do.

Leaving a good comment on a blog post. It is not enough to say that you liked someone's post or that you agreed with them. You need to say what you agreed, or disagreed and why, and offer reasons or competing evidence to support your position.

Examples of blog postings and comments.

Figure 5.3 is an example blog assignment. The idea is that there are well-crafted posts with comments from the class.

Here are examples of some great comments:

Kelly said . . . "I think your work really connects to the readings this week. Could you better explain what you mean by the challenges business faces with Big Data? I know Big Data presents challenges in terms for of its velocity and volume. However, I didn't quite understand what you meant by the variety of Big Data."

Frank said . . . "I think you really summarized the key points in reading for this week. It's amazing to hear that you've had experience working with Big Data. I think if businesses can harness the power of Big Data this will give them a competitive advantage. In your experience, how would a mid-size company get started with mining and analyzing Big Data?

Here are examples of not so good comments:

John said . . . "I really liked your post . . ."

Carrie said . . . "Well said."

Rohit said . . . "I disagree!"

Jessica said . . . "Me too!"

Figure 5.4 illustrates the professor's involvement in commenting on your work in a blog.

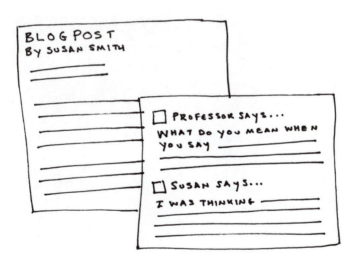

Figure 5.4 A blog posting with instructor questions

Try it!

5.2 Go to our website (http://savvyonlinestudent.com/tryit) and select blogs to try it out. You'll notice that typically, posts in a blog appear in chronological order—with the most recent post on top. You can try creating your own posting and/or commenting on a post by someone else. We encourage you to try both.

Working Collaboratively

Typically, when working with a group on a shared paper or project, you'll need a workspace. Use a collaborative tool to demonstrate and record your contributions and participation (see Chapter 6 for more on working in teams).

Tools that facilitate collaboration, such as wikis and Google Docs, allow for multiple people to contribute to a project. For example, in a wiki, it's easy to create new pages, establish links to existing ones, and assign "tags" or keywords to content. While a blog usually has a single author, a wiki is a collaboratively produced document. You probably are familiar with Wikipedia, the collaboratively written and edited encyclopedia with 4,110,000+ articles as of this writing. In a wiki, anyone can create or add content to a page. In class, wiki assignments could take multiple forms. You might:

- Author or update a page from Wikipedia.com based on your research.

- Create a class wiki on a particular topic or a glossary of terms.

- Use a wiki to mark up a literary text.

Another way to collaborate online is through Google Docs. Google Docs enable you to create the document and then share it with others. Document types include presentations, spreadsheets, and basic word processing. You and your group can create, revise, and edit the content. When you're ready you can share it with your professor and/or the class. You and your team members can even make comments on the document and revert back to earlier versions. The flexibility of working in a shared space removes barriers to version-control problems and multiple emails. The focus becomes the content rather than the management of that content.

Examples of Working Collaboratively

Figure 5.5 conceptually shows how wikis or collaborative online documents work. Teams can use these types of documents for administrative tasks such as project management of tasks. They're great for meeting agenda's and keeping meetings minutes to support the team web conferences. The teams could use the wiki to plan their interactions and decide who's doing what, by when. In addition, wikis work well for creating shared papers and reports. The key is that everyone can collaborate and edit.

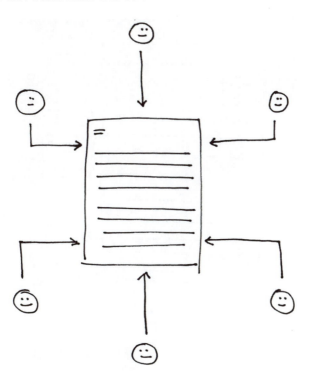

Figure 5.5 Multiple students working on a collaborative document or wiki

TIP

5.3 When working collaboratively on documents that can be edited by a distinct group of team members, set up some basic ground rules about who can edit what and when. Try to keep the rules simple and encourage everyone to contribute.

Another example is shown in Figure 5.6. This is a shared Google Doc, used to craft a final team report. The instructor and students can comment on the shared document along the way or use it to give feedback on the final product. The advantage to using Google Docs over wikis is that you can use the "add comment" function to ask questions, provide feedback. Document owners or collaborators then address those comments or respond in the context of the document itself.

Figure 5.6 Commenting on a shared Google Document

Try it!

5.3 Go to our website, http://savvyonlinestudent.com/tryit and select wiki to try it out. Then try contributing to our shared Google Doc. Also, review this video overview, *Google Docs in Plain English*, at: www.youtube.com/watch?v=eRqUE6IHTEA.

Meeting in Real Time

Your online course may have online meetings or "meet ups." These sessions work much like an on-site classroom, where you meet, live, in real time with your professor and classmates. Your professor leads the discussion and prompts the class for questions and feedback.

There are many conventions that govern discussions in physical classrooms, which vary depending upon the instructional goals, professor's preferences, course content, and class size. The format of small seminar, with students seated at a table, differs from that of a lecture in a large hall. The seminar table promotes discussion whereas asking a question in a lecture would be an interruption. How can one participate effectively in a virtual space?

Be prepared for the online class meeting—read the readings, have questions ready. Has your professor established norms for participating in the online class? What are they? It's arguably easier to be distracted in an online class. The temptation to check a social networking site could be great, and your peers cannot see that you have wandered off. Try to steel yourself against these distractions by signing out of them before you sign into your class. You may be unseen, but if your attention wanders off, you may not be ready when called upon to add to the discussion.

Listen carefully to what your peers are saying. Watch their webcams to see verbal cues. Follow the text-chat transcript if one is in use. Text chat can be a rich way to provide feedback and ask questions while class is in session, but keep your comments and questions on topic. At first, having to monitor a video stream, audio feed, supporting visuals, and text chat may seem overwhelming. In time, you will build your online participation muscles and get better at managing these streams:

Examples of online real-time meetings. The digital spaces where live sessions occur include LMS native tools and third-party tools such as Adobe Connect, Blackboard Collaborate, GoToMeeting, and WebEx, amongst others. In these environments, you can talk, be seen on camera, participate in the text chat, and use emoticons to provide emotional cues. You'll notice in Figure 5.7, a web-video conference where students are all on camera and can all see each other as well as the same document on their screens.

Many web-conferencing tools also enable real-time chats via text, in addition to talking into your microphone. See Figure 5.8 for an illustration.

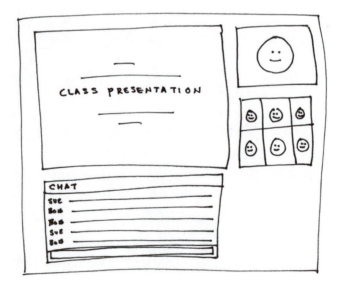

Figure 5.7 Live online class meeting

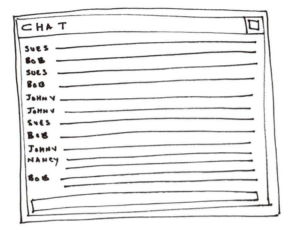

Figure 5.8 Real-time chat in an online course

Try it!

5.4 Go to our website, http://savvyonlinestudent.com/tryit to try out some of latest tools that are available. You'll need to ensure your computer has a video camera and a microphone.

Presenting

Presenting is a form of class participation. You are contributing to larger class dialogue through your contributions. Moreover, as an audience member observing other's participation, your role is to raise questions, offer suggestions, and provide feedback.

You can create presentations to demonstrate your work to your professor and your peers. Usually, presentations are abbreviated versions of a project or report. Consult resources on how to make an effective presentation, such as Seth Godin's *Really Bad PowerPoint* (www.sethgodin.com/freeprize/reallybad-1.pdf). Know your audience and to help them understand your message.

The format for a presentation in an online class presentation ranges from a live web cast to a simple slide show using PowerPoint. Either you, or you and your teammates, present on a topic. Then, seek feedback from the instructor and your peers. If presenting asynchronously, you could post a simple slide presentation in PowerPoint. Better yet, you could post a narrated screencast that displays your PowerPoint in a way that the slides transition with your narration. Finally, you could produce an audio recording of a speech for a communications course. Consult the requirements and guidelines for your course.

Examples of Student Presentations

Figure 5.9 is an example of a group presentation delivered via video. These students used Google Presentations to create a slideshow. They embedded the presentation into a blog, to allow for comments by the professor and peers. Another approach, is to record a video over a slideshow and share it.

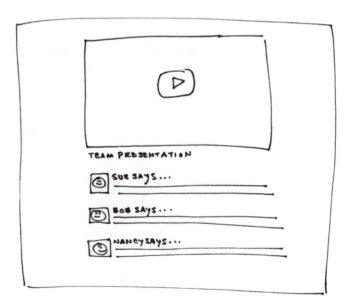

Figure 5.9 Online recorded student video presentation with student comments

Finally, you may be asked to review a presentation by your instructor. Typically, this includes a recorded video presentation with an option to ask questions and make comments. Those comments can be made in the native tool the video is produced in, such as YouTube. Also, there's typically a place to link/embed the video in the LMS.

Try it!

5.5 Go to our website and select our sample presentations to observe. Next, try building a quick presentation following our instructions.

Making Thoughtful Class Contributions

Critical thinking is the art of analyzing and evaluating thinking with a view to improving it.

—Elder, Paul, and Hiler, *Thinker's Guide Series*

It may seem obvious that your contributions to online class dialogue should be thoughtful and engaging. However, repeated studies (see, for example, Arum and Roksa in *Academically Adrift*) show that undergraduate students at U.S. institutions are not improving key skills such as complex reasoning, critical thinking and writing. Rigorous participation in online classes builds these skills. Apply critical thinking to your process of participating in a discussion forum, live class meeting, or even when reflecting on your work.

Takeaways

— Understand what expectations are for your online class participation.

— Craft thoughtful well-written responses and feedback.

— Respond to your professor and peers in a timely fashion via online discussions.

Participating in Your Online Course

— Try using the various technologies for participation, such as discussion forums, web-conferencing tools, blogs, wikis, etc.

— Know your audience for an online presentation.

Chapter 6

Working in Teams

Virtual team activities help bring learners together to sort out problems and engage in deeper discussion.

—Pratt and Palloff, *Collaborating Together*

Teamwork is not easy.

—Volchok, "Building better virtual teams"

Just as in any other course, you may work in groups. The main difference is that in an online course you'll work in a virtual team. When working in a team, it's your responsibility to contribute to the team goals and work together to achieve the objectives set out by your instructor. In this chapter, we'll provide you with some guidelines for working in virtual teams.

Group Objectives and Activities

Your professor sets the objectives of your team. Your team's responsibility is to meet those objectives. Typical team activities include discussions, presentations, projects, papers, case studies, debates, wikis, and so on.

When reading through group assignments, determine if it's the product or the process that's the most important outcome of the project. If you haven't seen a sample team activity, refer to the example below. This activity speaks more to process, since the assignment is about providing feedback on the team progress of the team.

Team Activity

The purpose of this activity is to share your project progress with the class and receive feedback from the other teams. To do that, share your project framework and comment on the frameworks posted by others.

Part A: In the week 4 discussion forum, one person from each team should provide a brief outline of the Li and Bernoff's POST (People, Objectives, Strategy, and Technology) framework that will guide the implementation of your project. To go above and beyond, state the success measures for each objective.

Complete this before 7/31 to give other teams an opportunity to comment.

Part B: Comment on the frameworks shared by the other teams. Comments should go beyond "this is great," and focus on the strategies and success measures. Teams are encouraged to moderate the discussion, and to respond to questions and comments directed at their projects.

Types of Groups and Forming Teams

Creating groups typically takes two forms: (1) instructors make assignments based on criteria, for example, students having different skills; or (2) instructors make group assignments at random; or (3) students can self organize. If you are asked to form your own team, you'll have to be very pro-active in recruiting team members. For this Sandy Pentland advises, "The best way to build a great team is to not select individuals for their smarts or accomplishments but learn how they communicate." Look for students that have been active in class to date. This may give you insights into their behavior as a team member. If a student is individually inactive in your course, that person is probably not going to be a dynamic team member. Also, review the online profiles of your peers to learn more about their skills, background, and written communication style (see Chapter 3).

> TIP
>
> **6.1 Start talking with your team as soon as you can.**
> It's best to start out by meeting the members of your team in a live online meeting. Refer to Chapter 2 for more details on conducting a web conference.

You'll most likely work in a group in which everyone has a different set of skills but shares a common knowledge base. This is based on your academic training, the program you are in, or the class learning outcomes. The advantage of working in heterogeneous teams is that different perspectives can be shared. The disadvantage is that there may not be a shared level of expertise by two or more team members.

Making Your Online Team Work

There are several elements that are required to assemble great online team:

1. **An understanding of the objectives**. Each member of the team should know the objectives and outcomes of the assigned project. Michael Ryan developed a quick checklist for virtual team members:

Virtual Team Member Checklist

☐ Embrace diversity.

☐ Be proactive.

☐ Don't dilute the value of communication. Recognize the value of good judgement.

☐ Explore the team vision and goals. Recognize their value to the ultimate success of the team and each member.

Source: Virtual Teamwork: Mastering the Art and Practice of Online Learning and Corporate Collaboration, (2010)

63

2. **A project manager**. The team needs to nominate, or someone needs to volunteer, to lead your team. The project manager can help the team organize its time, milestones, and tasks to achieve the desired outcomes. Some group projects require a rotating team leader and/or project manager.

3. **Appropriate use of project management tools**. Some projects require tracking of milestones and tasks. Project management tools help in accountability of tasks. However, they're best used for longer-term projects (a full semester) rather than for shorter, week-long projects.

4. **Appropriate selection and use of communication tools**. The team should agree on using email, Skype, and so on, to get in touch and stay in touch with one another.

5. **Use of collaboration spaces to share work and progress on team deliverables**. Members in virtual teams need a workspace to share the progress of their work with one another. Google docs, the LMS workspace, and Dropbox are just some options.

While these are just a few tips for success, it's important to recognize that team building is not instantaneous. Bruce Tuckman and Mary Ann Jensen provide a useful framework to analyze and track the stages of your team development (see Figure 6.1). This framework illustrates the path to high-performing teams.

The first stage, forming, begins with the team objectives and a team charter. Next, issues are highlighted early in the storming stage of team development. This is when team members compete for recognition of their ideas. However, while this process can be

FORMING > STORMING > NORMING > PERFORMING > ADJOURNING

Figure 6.1 The five stages of team development and evolution

contentious, it's essential to the development of the team. During the norming stage, the team has shared goals, and members take responsibly for their work. In the performing stage you'll begin to see positive results for your team's collective efforts. Finally, the adjourning stage is when you've completed your work as a team.

> TIP
>
> **6.2 Establish a team charter.** A useful resource for this stage is available at: www.mindtools.com/pages/article/newTMM_95.htm.

A variety of factors, such as trust, shared goals, and motivation contribute to the health of any team. According to the research by Pentland and the MIT Human Dynamics Laboratory, energy level and engagement are the most important predictors of a team's success. In other words, for your team to be successful it's best to meet often, for all members to contribute, and for team members to engage with other teams in the class.

Your Group Workspace

In your online course, the LMS should have a space for group work. Each LMS describes the space a little differently, but the functions are the same: it can be called *Work Groups*, *Groups*, *Teamwork*, and so on. Your instructor creates your team workspace in the LMS. See Figure 6.2 for an example.

At times, these workspaces can actually impede group collaboration. They are tools for communication, but they tend to lack the tools needed for your group project.

Another shortcoming of LMS based group tools is the lack of project management tools. Typically, when working on a collaborative project, calendaring and task management tools help. Consider setting up a

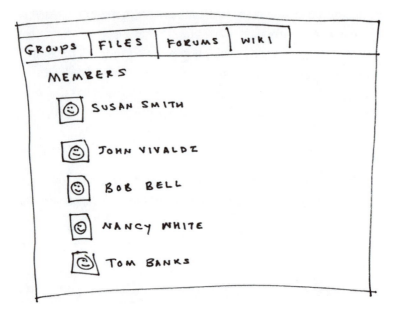

Figure 6.2 An example of an online group workspace in an LMS

6.3 Build a shared online team calendar to manage tasks and deadlines.

Google Calendar for your team meetings and deadlines. Also, there are some free project management tools, such as Trello or Basecamp, that could be helpful as well.

TIP

6.4 Use collaborative authoring tools. In addition to the workspace provided by your school's LMS, consider using Google Apps for Collaboration. Google Docs, Presentations, and Spreadsheets allow for multi-user authoring and creation of content. It's great for writing reports, drafting presentations, and managing projects.

When Working in Teams Doesn't Work

Teams don't always work well together. Reasons include the lack of motivation from team members, the lack of a shared cause or goal, and the mismanagement of the team building process. According to Morten Hansen, a noted authority on teams, "bad collaboration is worse than no collaboration." Poor collaboration not only happens in the classroom but also in the workplace. Some common pitfalls include:

Collaborating in hostile territory. The course and the surrounding environs need to be equipped to collaborate. This means having the right tools, a good attitude, and clear understanding of the team objectives. You, your teammates, and professor need to support the collaborative efforts.

Over-collaborating. Make sure team meetings are set with an agenda and purpose. Brainstorming meetings are useful, but the team is expected to produce as well. Ensure each team member has responsibilities.

Overshooting potential value. It's possible that you and your team will think you can achieve and produce much more than you can. Be sure goals are realistic and understand the limitations of your teammates.

Underestimating the costs. There may be times, at the expense of your own learning, when you may be required to work in a team. The team may be less knowledgeable or skilled than you. In this case, you'll be in a position to teach and lead even if you may gain little in terms of actual content knowledge. Nevertheless, teaching is a great way to refine your knowledge.

Misdiagnosing the problem. There are barriers to collaboration that include the team itself and the team members' different levels of content expertise in the

67

subject you're studying. Be sure that when forming and working with your team, attention is paid to both.

Implementing the wrong solution. Tools are not a substitute for leadership. Setting up a shared workspace (i.e. Google Docs) may help the team function, but tools are only part of the process. Avoid this trap by defining team roles clearly.

There should be a common reason why a team is working together: Together team members should be able to achieve something that would otherwise be impossible but make sure that everyone is engaged. There need to be benefits for all.

Confrontations

At some point while taking an online course, conflict will arise. Conflict is a part of life and different people handle confrontation in different ways. Some avoid it. Some seek it out. For example, you may have a deep disagreement with a classmate over what direction to take on a group project. You may be dissatisfied with your team's grade on an assignment. In these situations, it's often worth addressing the conflict so that it can be resolved. If you are not skilled at confrontation, here are a few pointers:

Consider the medium. Be aware of the subtleties of the medium that you are using. "Cooler" mediums, such as email, are easily misinterpreted. Tone and humor may not be understood by the recipient as intended.

Review your communications. Before sending what could be interpreted as a heated email, try reading it aloud. What do you notice about your tone? Or your own feelings? A phone conversation re-introduces the tone of your voice, but still leaves your partner without visual feedback. Skype, or your institution's virtual classroom, may allow you to see one another.

Try to talk in real time. When there's a chance for things to be misunderstood, simply ask for a phone or web meeting to discuss the issues at hand.

Here's a sample student email message that works well for addressing team issues:

Hi Shivani: I am a bit worried about the upcoming deadline for Project 1. Would you have a few minutes to discuss this week? I have time available on Wednesday at 5 p.m. or Friday a.m. Might either of these work for you?

Looking forward to speaking with you.

Samantha

In this example, Samantha shared what she's concerned about, and set up a time to talk. She also set an agenda so that Shivani can bring ideas about how to address that deadline.

Team Assessment and Feedback

When teamwork is integral to the learning process, your professor may ask you to evaluate one another and the team as a whole. See Figure 6.3 for an example of a peer evaluation that an instructor may

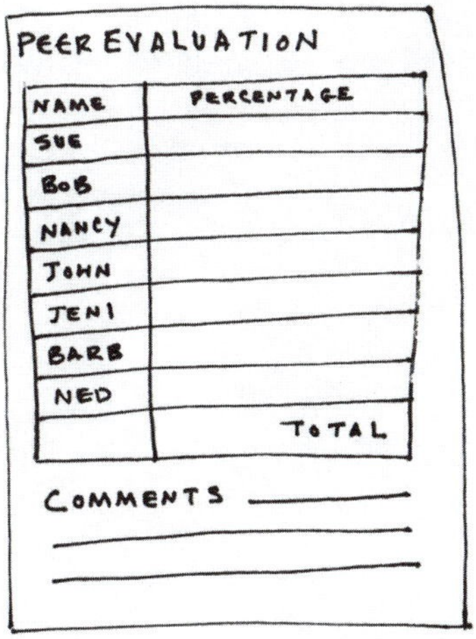

Figure 6.3 A sample peer evaluation form for group project work

ask you to complete. These evaluations usually involve allocating a percentage to each team member that represents their contribution to the team as a whole. For example, if there were four team members including yourself, and each team member contributed equally, each member would be allocated 25 percent. Uneven distributions provide a signal to your instructor of how well the team worked together and who contributed more or less.

Check the class syllabus; sometimes these evaluations will be factored into your grade. Be prepared to give and accept constructive feedback. Team evaluations often come at the end of the course. Our advice: don't wait to offer feedback that can help your team work better. Feedback is best when it is timely, specific and actionable. For example:

> Maria, I was inspired by how passionate you were when you defended Anton's actions when he confronted his boss in the case study. You also cited specific examples from our management text. Could you lead that section of our presentation?

Finally, here are questions to help you get feedback and construct a team evaluation:

- What worked particularly well?

- What could have worked better?

- How did it feel to be a member of the team?

- How was the process of working together?

- What collaboration was particularly effective? Why?

- How well did the group use tools to aid in collaboration? Did they help or hinder?

- What about the product? How good was it? How did team members feel about it? Were there some parts that were better than others?

- How well did the team do at defining roles and responsibilities? How well was work apportioned among team members?

- Were team members able to develop new skills?

- How well structured was the assignment? How could it have been better designed to improve team dynamics and the project's deliverable?

- How did the team's product compare to the work of other teams?

These questions will help you move beyond non-critical feedback responses, such as "my team members worked together well or poorly."

Takeaways

— Make an effort to meet your team members early.

— Clarify objectives and tasks with your team members and professor.

— Designate a leader. Consider rotating that leader through the course, if applicable.

— Select the appropriate collaboration, communication, project management tools for the project and team.

— Communicate with team members to resolve problems quickly and effectively.

— Give critical and helpful feedback.

— Be honest on your peer evaluations.

Chapter 7

Individual Work

In earlier chapters, we discussed the online group and participation activities. In this chapter, we tackle the work that you do on your own. In some ways, it has the most in common with its analog equivalent, homework. You've been doing some form of homework as a part of your education for some time. When done right, these independent activities reinforce your learning and allow you to become more familiar with new content and concepts. Online individual work serves the same function. The key difference here is that instead of using older technology—paper and ink—you use newer tools to work on and submit assignments. By the time you finish this chapter, you will have a good sense of the different kinds of individual work that you may encounter in your online studies, and be knowledgeable about how to approach it.

Reading, Listening, and Viewing

Whether online or on-site, reading comprises the core part of the academic experience. In your online studies, you encounter the same kinds of content: novels, textbooks, data sets, and more. Sometimes your readings will be on paper—we assume that you are familiar with how to read and annotate in that format. When learning online, many of your materials are digital, which means you use digital tools, such as a PDF reader, to highlight and annotate those documents. The same basic rules apply when reading online as when reading on paper. Read with purpose and take notes. Modern PDF readers have built in highlighting and note taking tools. Mark passages and make notes that are important to your studies. In addition to saving trees, there are other advantages to going digital. It is easier to collect highlighted passages on a digital PDF for inclusion and citation in a paper. In Chapter 2, we discussed eReaders and tablets—reading and annotating works well on those devices. Tools like Mendeley make it easy to keep track of a range of scholarly sources, and to link your notes with those sources. Still, if you do not feel comfortable reading on a computer or tablet, print your documents.

> **TIP**
>
> **7.1 Use a bookmark manager to keep track of interesting things you read or sources for class.**
> Zotero, Mendeley, and Diigo all make tracking and sharing what you find online easy.

Professors often assign videos as "texts" for class—they may be lectures, panels, TV shows, or film segments. Approach these multimedia texts with the same critical eye that you would the printed word. Tune out other distractions. Have a note-taking strategy. When you are reading a passage that you do not understand, you are able to go back. The same applies when you are watching or listening to videos. Get comfortable using the playback controls so that you can go back and review important sections. Use note-taking tools that work for you.

Figure 7.1 Take notes while watching an online video lecture, as you would if you were attending a face-to-face lecture

7.2 **Make notes that refer to audio or video time-codes**,
e.g., "Bladerunner, 0:04m:11ss, we meet Deckard, the
self-assured, cocky cop."

Reviewing and Completing Your Assignments

Refer to Table 7.1 for a list of different assignments and their
purposes. These assignments represent a range of possibilities.
Familiarize yourself with the tactics and purpose of each assignment
type. For details, refer to the course syllabus, where, you will find the
assignments, grade percentages, and due dates. Your professor may
or may not provide a detailed description for each assignment in
advance. Instead, she may include those details in a separate section
or release it later in an announcement to the class.

Table 7.1 Online assignment types and how to submit them
online

Assignment Type	Description and Purpose	Tactics
Self Assessment	These tools allow you to check what you know about a topic and are usually ungraded.	Answer honestly—the feedback you get will be more useful.
Reflections	These assignments allow you to connect what you are learning to your prior knowledge, and to learn better as a result.	Get comfortable writing in your own voice. Write freely and resist editing as you go. Consider your audience—is your posting for a class blog, your professor, or yourself?

continued

Table 7.1 *continued*

Assignment Type	Description and Purpose	Tactics
Games and Simulations	Though it depends upon the game or simulation, you are immersed in an activity, and given a role: saving a life, overseeing a refugee camp, etc. These tools help build decision-making skills in an authentic, but lower stakes environment.	Try to understand the game or simulation's underlying purpose. Are you trying to solve a problem? Learn a new skill? Play. After a session, think about what you learned.
Presentations (Individual)	Individual presentations allow you to share your knowledge of a given topic with your professor and peers.	Develop a solid outline. Use stories, relevant examples, and visuals to get your point across. Rehearse until you feel comfortable with the material.
Case Studies	Case studies promote analytical thinking and problem solving skills. They are open ended, and therefore offer many possible answers or approaches to problems.	Read or review case materials thoroughly. Identify the core issues and problems. If your instructor offers framing questions, use them as a point of departure. Develop an opinion about the subject matter and prepare a defense if challenged.
Papers	The purpose of papers varies from class to class, but usually a paper is written to show mastery of a particular content area.	Start writing early. Develop an outline. Partner up with a reader to review early drafts.

continued overleaf

Table 7.1 *continued*

Assignment Type	Description and Purpose	Tactics
Problem Sets	Used to assess quantitative skills in economics, statistics, and other classes based on math.	Begin with easier problems first. Break a problem down into smaller parts. Look at a range of completed examples. Take advantage of your faculty member's office hours.
Textbook Supplements	A printed textbook is static while online sources are sometimes dynamic. These supplements expand on, or update, what is in the book, and may include problem sets or examples.	Use them—they may be more up to date than the book itself, and help give you an edge.

Submitting Assignments

Once you have completed your work, you will need to give it to your professor or peers for review. One of the most common ways to submit work is via a drop box—a secure file folder to which you and your professor have access. Navigate to the folder for a given assignment and upload it.

If you have trouble using the drop box, email your instructor the assignment instead, or post it to a location, such as Google Docs, where it can be easily retrieved.

Scanning Your Work

Sometimes, you may not use digital tools to create your work. Pencil and paper remain powerful tools to express ideas quickly and easily. Perhaps you have been asked to share sketches in a drawing class or the steps you took when solving a math problem. In these cases, it is simpler to scan your work and then upload it to your course. Scanners were once specialized tools. Today, they are included in multifunction printers and exist as apps on smart phones.

A Few Tips for Submitting Assignments

- Submit on time. LMSs will date and time stamp your work—some drop boxes may even lock after the assignment due date.

- Put your name in the filename and on the assignment itself. Example: "TaraJones_Assignment01."

- Use a format that makes it easy to comment and annotate, e.g., Word, Google Docs, or PDF, or the file format assigned for a particular class. For a photography class, your professor might want to see layered Photoshop files, but that would probably not be an appropriate format for your art history class.

Home office multi-function printers usually have a one-button scan feature that generates a PDF document. Your office copier might also be smarter than you think. See if it has a scan feature. Though not as convenient, these so-called "flatbed" scanners solve the problem of adequate light and produce better scans than smart phones. You could still draw that sketch of a great idea on a cocktail napkin, snap a picture with your smartphone and share it with a classmate.

7.3 How to get a good scan with a mobile phone:

- Place the document on a flat surface.
- Ensure the object you are scanning is well lit (soft light, preferably indirect is best).
- Take a picture.
- Zoom in to make sure the text or lines are clear.
- Crop out anything that should not be in the frame.

Sharing Big Files

If you are working in a class where you are producing digital content, such as a workshop on video editing, the files that you produce will be large. In these cases, consider using a peer-to-peer (P2P) file service. These tools let you send a file directly from your computer to another via a customized link. Search for "peer to peer file sharing": www.justbeamit.com, www.pipebytes.com, www.yousendit.com, and www.mediafire.com are good options. Do an internet search first though. New tools are always being developed.

Taking Quizzes, Tests, and Exams

Just mentioning the word test or exam strikes fear in the hearts of some students. The best way to prepare for any type of test is to do the work as you go. Familiarize yourself with the testing tools, so that they are not new on the day that you are taking the exam or quiz.

In the context of an LMS, a test is just a form, and much like its paper predecessor: you fill it out and turn it in. Assessments may be timed, so make a note of when you start. Some institutions make use of virtual proctoring tools, which may record your actions while taking an exam. Generally, searching for answers during a limited test time is not an effective strategy. However, ask your professor before the test if it is allowable to use your notes or other materials as an aid for answering questions.

> TIP
>
> **7.4 When taking an online exam that requires a response to an essay question, compose your response in a text editor.** This ensures that if you lose your internet connection or the system fails, you'll have a back up of your responses. Save your work early and often. When you are done, cut and paste it into the web form.

What About Math?

Keyboards are designed to get words and numbers into a computer. Things get a bit more complicated when you are working with mathematical formulae. How you enter and work with formulae will depend upon your class and your instructor. Table 7.2 provides common approaches for your consideration.

Table 7.2 Common mathematical notation tools

Approach	Benefits	Drawbacks
Hand write notation; scan and upload solutions.	Focus on the problem, and its component parts instead of how to render the notion.	Legibility may be a problem.
Render the formulae in a program like Word or Google Docs. Try it. http://goo.gl/MezgO.	You choose from a pre-set vocabulary of symbols.	Formulae are limited to that format, and may not easily convert to another.
Use numeric input for mathematical symbols.	Easy—uses the keyboard for input.	The symbols look different from those we see in a text or on a virtual board. It takes some getting used to.
Use a web-based program like MathJax.	No downloads required; works in any browser. Lots of support within Math communities.	Designed for presenting content on the web. Requires some modest coding skills.
Use Math ML to render the formulae.	The official (W3C) standard for rendering math on the web.	Relatively complex code. It takes time to learn how to render symbols.
Equation editor in the LMS.	Easy—uses the keyboard for input.	May only available within specific applications in the LMS, such as test entry boxes.

There are many specialized tools for studying math—Mathematica, and its web companion, Wolfram Alpha, www.wolframalpha.com, are worth exploring if you are or aspire to be a math geek.

What About Languages?

If you're taking a foreign language course, you'll probably have to type up your assignments using characters unique to your keyboard. To enter text in another language, activate the keyboard for that particular language. However, if you are only working with a few words, then using a word processor's, "Insert > Symbol" feature is a plausible tactic.

Let's say that we want to render the sentence, "I'd like to go to Munich tomorrow."

Ich möchte am morgen nach München fahren.

To get this result, we simply went to translate.google.com, and entered the English phrase. Google returned a machine translation.

Perhaps we are writing a paper on Soviet newspapers, and want to show *Pravda* ('*Truth*') in all its Cyrillic glory:

правда

All of this is possible because of the miracle of Unicode. Thanks to this technology standard, it's easier than ever for computers to render text in just about any language. Mac OS, Windows, and Linux all have good Unicode support. For more, visit Penn State's excellent page: http://tlt.its.psu.edu/suggestions/international/web/unicode.html. You will find details on working with characters from other languages, as well as how to install a new keyboard map if you are doing extensive writing in a different language.

Producing Videos or Podcasts

When the web was in its infancy, producing video and audio recording required specialized equipment. Today, most of us walk around with devices that are capable of recording audio and video. The web provides the infrastructure to easily upload and share our creations. Your assignments in online courses could consist of producing a podcast or video podcast, where you record yourself speaking on an assigned topic.

There are many tools to produce these projects. Here are some of the more popular tools for those starting out with sound and video editing:

Video and audio editing tools. Table 7.3 presents common audio/video tools for creating and editing for PC, Mac, and Linux systems.

Sometimes it is useful to record the contents of your screen with a narration as well. For example, you may want to show how a fellow student how to make an array formula in Excel. A picture may be worth 1,000 words, but a video, showing you how to solve a problem step-by-step, can be even more valuable. The same steps for producing a screencast apply to producing a video:

Sharing your video and audio creations. Video files tend to be large. There are many options for uploading and sharing your videos, but our favorite is YouTube.

Table 7.3 Audio/video editing tools

Platform	Audio	Video
Mac	Garage Band, Audacity	Photobooth, iMovie, Screenflow
PC	Audacity	Windows Movie Maker, Magix Movie Edit Pro, Camtasia
Linux	Audacity	Advidemux

Video/Audio Workflow

Brainstorm—what are you trying to accomplish with your recording?

Storyboard—what are the specific things you are trying to cover? Think of this as an outline, but with pictures along with words.

Shoot/Record—you can use your webcam, smart phone or a digital camcorder.

Edit—take out what you don't want or that doesn't tell the story.

Share—put your masterpiece someplace that others, whether your instructor or the other students, can access it.

It's possible to add captions, edit your video and even decide who gets to share it. Creating a YouTube Channel of your own work could be a part of your online profile or ePortfolio. Vimeo is a solid alternative. For audio files, SoundCloud is a good choice. Once you have posted your project in a place where your professor and peers can find it, post a link to your LMS. Your professor should provide more detailed instructions.

Writing Papers

7.5 **Use track changes.** Modern word processing tools make it easy for other readers to comment on and edit your work. Your professor may use these tools to provide feedback on a paper. You can also enable these tools to show your professor how a draft evolved.

You are familiar with writing papers, whether they are essays or longer research papers. Your classes will have details about how to approach a particular assignment. The process of writing and

Figure 7.2 The process of submitting and receiving feedback on papers in an online course

receiving feedback from your professor and peers may take a form as illustrated in Figure 7.2.

Here are a few tips to make your work easily accessible to your faculty and peers. Your professor may have specific instructions that override these recommendations:

- Include your name, and a reference to the assignment in the file name, for example, Smith_Lit101_Paper1.

- Include your name on the first page.

- Use page numbers.

- Use standard margins, 1 inch on each side of the page.

- Use a single, standard font, such as Helvetica or Times New Roman, 12 point.

The idea is that the focus should be on your words, not the formatting. There are excellent tips for writing at Purdue's Online Writing Lab, also known as OWL: http://owl.english.purdue.edu/owl/.

Takeaways

— Familiarize yourself with the types of individual assignments required for your course.

— Understand the requirements for those individual assignments, tests, and quizzes that you'll be expected to complete.

Individual Work

— Know the tools necessary for completing your assignments.

— Entering formulae or special characters is possible, but requires additional effort.

— Test tools for assignments or assessments in advance to avoid a crunch.

Chapter 8

Evaluating Performance

Self deception is the worst deception.

—Plato

If you don't know where you're going, you just might get there.

—Yogi Berra

Examinations are formidable even to the best prepared, for the greatest fool may ask more than the wisest man can answer.

—Charles Caleb Colton

> In the previous chapters, we discussed the elements that make up an online course, from blogs to team projects to wikis. In this chapter, we discuss evaluation. As an online student, it's important to have a good sense of how you are doing in your course or program. You will leave this chapter with a sense of how evaluation works online—from how your instructors review and grade your work, to self or peer assessments.

You are no stranger to the concept of evaluating your academic performance. Educational systems around the globe measure student progress. Students take tests and complete assignments. Instructors award grades, to indicate that you have reached a certain performance threshold. Individual assignment grades culminate in an overall grade for a course. Institutions compile course grades and calculate grade point averages. Upstart education providers or programs award badges, which demonstrate mastery of a particular subject, sub-topic or skill.

Why Evaluate?

Feedback helps us grow and makes us aware of what we know. It speaks to accomplishments and shortcomings, and aids us as we fill gaps and build new skills. Grades also signal to you and others how well you did. As you think through the "why" of evaluation, consider these different perspectives and their essential questions:

Table 8.1 Evaluation perspectives and essential questions

Perspective	Essential Questions
Self	How am I doing? Am I learning? How well? Am I acquiring new skills? What are they? How well do I apply them? Where did I begin? Where did I end up? Where do I go from here? What are my goals for this course or program? Why am I taking this course? What grade do I want to earn? What am I willing to do to get it?
Peers	How knowledgeable are the other students? What was their contribution? How much did _____ learn during the educational experience? How well did our team work at completing its assignment? How do I think my classmates are doing? How is my team performing? What do they think of my performance?
Instructor	Instructor: Are my students engaged? Are my students meeting the learning objectives? At what level are they now? Where would I like them to be at the end of the term? How is my teaching? Grades that an instructor awards identify the gap between what you think you know and what an expert thinks you know given how well you did on a given assignment.
Program/ World	How well are the students learning? Is our institutional mission being fulfilled? How well do students know the subject? How do we know that you know? What are students now qualified to do that they were not qualified to do before?

How is Evaluation Similar to What I Have Already Experienced As a Student or As a Professional in the Workplace?

In online courses and programs, evaluation tends to be formal compared to the feedback that you might get on a job. At work, assignments are frequent, but grades may be issued just once a year in the form of an annual performance review. Just as with their on-site counterparts, assignment grades lead to course grades, which culminate in a grade point average, and eventually to a degree, diploma, or certificate.

How Does Evaluation Differ Online?

Online instructors avail themselves of the learning environment to provide automatic, sometimes instant, feedback to students. As a student, you may take various tests—multiple choice, one word answer, matching or true-false—and get a score as soon as you submit your work. More advanced assessments adapt to how you answer questions and provide easier or more difficult questions to help you practice. Self-study tutorials, like those found on Khan Academy, provide this sort of adaptive feedback. Instructors in online classes may only make new content available after you have scored a certain level on a test or quiz, or completed a series of steps.

In a similar vein, because all work is digital and requires the use of communication tools, it is relatively easy to assess both the assignment and the process you use complete it. For example, let's say that you are working on a team project. Your instructor assigns you to a group, and then requires your team to conduct virtual meetings and record them. She offers feedback on what worked well about the meeting and what did not. Your instructor could also require you and your team to post and share meeting minutes and action items. Newer tools for creating documents, such as Google Docs, allow an instructor to see who contributed what sections, who made comments, and how an assignment came together.

Other modern communications tools, such as instant messaging and email, make it very easy to collaborate and share answers. They may facilitate collaboration, but they can also aid cheating. Imagine a scenario where an instructor gives an online quiz to a class. The instructor sets the quiz to close a week later. Students copy and paste questions and answers to specific questions, or search the web for answers. They might find previous students made and shared a digital copy of an exam. Students use this copy as a study guide for the exam, and memorize the answers. Because it is easier for students to game assessments today, professors need to come up with methods for assessing knowledge and skills that are less susceptible to cheating.

In online courses, feedback you get is a key instructional strategy—in other words, much of the teaching happens in the responses you get to your work. In well-designed courses, you get frequent feedback not only from your instructors, but also from your peers, and maybe even from outside experts or the world at large. All of these interactions can add up to a super-charged learning experience.

How Professors Decide What to Evaluate

In your online courses, assessment depends on the course's learning objectives. For example, if the course is focused on improving student writing, then providing feedback to students about their writing will be one of the core assessments. If courses cover particular content areas, then demonstrating mastery of those areas—for example, the causes of World War II in the course "20th Century Warfare" would be paramount. If you are learning how to create data visualizations, then rating the efficacy of those visualizations will be a key factor in assessments. Here is an example of learning outcomes in a data visualization course, see box opposite.

Review your course syllabus for the learning outcomes to ensure you know what you are supposed to be able to do by the end of your course.

Learning Outcomes

- Understand and apply strategies of analytical design.

- Identify appropriate data visualization techniques given particular requirements imposed by the data.

- Analyze and critique examples of visualizations.

- Interpret meaning from multidimensional formats and presentation techniques.

- Use techniques learned to generate visualizations appropriate to the specific audience type, task, and data source.

- Create multiple versions of digital visualizations using various software packages.

An example of course learning outcomes

What Instructors Wish Students Knew and Appreciated about Evaluation

It's not easy to design effective assessments. Creating assessments is time-consuming. Instructors may struggle with creating instruments that accurately measure what students have learned:

Cheating is a problem. It's arguably never been easier to cheat, and, online, assessments are often not observed by a third party. Students can post the answers to a test, or a strategy for gaming an assessment, and share it with others. When it is discovered the instructor may have to create a new assessment. Policing plagiarism is also challenging. Following up on academic integrity complaints takes time away from teaching, research, and other work.

New assessments must be designed, developed, implemented, graded, and refined. Exam questions or quiz items have to be written, tested, and reworked.

Giving students candid critical feedback is a skill that instructors develop over time. Some are better at it than others.

It can be boring. We try to vary assignments in our classes so that we're not reading the same topics again and again. Assessment is more rewarding when a student has a fresh, yet well informed, perspective on a topic.

How are different categories of activities evaluated in online courses? One of the benefits of the digital medium is that it captures many student interactions along the way. Consider these categories of assignments, the tools that you may encounter, and tips on how to make the most of each.

TIP

8.1 Ask for more time early if circumstances warrant it.
During your online studies, there may be a time when you are overwhelmed, in spite of good planning. When this happens, write a note to your instructor in advance of a deadline, to see if more time might be possible. It's better to ask before the assignment is due. State your case. If your reasons are compelling, an instructor may be willing to grant an extension. Notifying instructors of late submissions is also good practice.

How Do Professors Grade Your Assignments?

The kind of assignment determines the grading strategy. In the table below, we review common categories of assignments and how instructors may grade them. These are general approaches. Be sure to check your course syllabus and learn about how your work will be assessed in your class.

Table 8.2 Assignment categories, online tools, and tips

Assignment Category	Online Tools	Tips
Participation	Blogs Forums Wikis Comments Server logs: logins, time spent in course	Sign in frequently. Make timely, thoughtful and incisive contributions. Respond to your peers. Don't wait until the last minute.
Subject Matter Knowledge	Exams Tests Quizzes Essays Problem sets Research papers	Keep up with the work. Develop your own mini-assessments: the process of asking yourself questions and providing the answers helps you rehearse what you know and encode the knowledge into your long term memory. Form an online study group to ask one another questions.
Mastery of a New Skill	Presentations Projects Demonstrations of new skills	Building new skills takes time and practice. Fail early, fail often, and fail better. Get feedback from peers and experts. Consider recording yourself and posting online to solicit relevant feedback.

Table 8.3 Assignment types and how instructors grade them

Assignment Type	How Instructors May Grade it
Papers	How well did the paper address the assigned topic? Quality of content, arguments, research, grammar and usage.
Presentations	Clarity, relevance, persuasion, and impact. Quality of visuals, delivery, responses to questions and answers.
Group Projects	Assessment of work product, such as the deliverables, e.g., a marketing plan, or the process itself, or both. You might receive a team grade, or individual grade, or both. Instructors may call upon peers to evaluate one another and the group as a whole.
Blog Posts	Insightfulness of post, how well the post brings in the class readings, and connects what's being learned with prior experience.
Forum Discussions	Quality of ideas, substance, and frequency of contributions. Responses to peers and ability to stay on topic.
Content Mastery	Exams, tests, quizzes, essay questions. Oral presentations or talks about a particular topic.
New Skills	Demonstrations of new skills with a scale that shows how well a particular sub-skill is mastered.
Problem Sets	According to an answer key—typically scored as number right. Instructors may award partial credit for answers that are incorrect, but that have effective reasoning.

Grading

What all of these assignments have in common is that your professor will award you grades for the work that you do. The instructor has data on how you as an individual did on an assignment, and also how the class as a whole performed. Though there are regulations in the United States that prohibit instructors from sharing individual student grades, instructors may choose to provide a grade distribution—how many students earned an A, B, or C—or perhaps share the assignment's average score. This data can help a student understand how well he performed relative to his peers. All online classes are different, but what they all have in common is that they have assignments. Professors combine assignments into categories. See Table 8.3 for example of different assignment types and how instructors may grade those assignments.

How Do You Learn about Your Grades?

In an on-site course, professors return papers or homework in the classroom at the beginning of a session or perhaps offer feedback to the class as a whole. Online, instructors use the course's grade book to disseminate this vital information. (See Figure 8.1 for an example of how it looks.) The grade book lets you see how you did on an individual assignment and your performance over time.

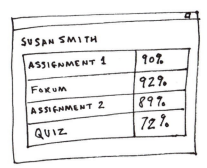

Figure 8.1 An example of an online grade book where you can find your grades and track your progress

Badges—an Alternative to Grades

If you grew up as a Boy or Girl Scout, the concept of badges— wearing a fabric patch to show that you had a certain skill—is familiar to you. These badges have taken on a digital form, but they still show mastery of a particular skill or content area. For example, Code Academy, a web site that teaches people how to write computer programs, awards different badges as students complete challenges. The idea is that you can display similar badges on your online profile to signify to employers that you have expertise in a particular area.

When and How to Appeal a Grade

There may come a time when you think that the grade an instructor awarded you for a particular assignment, or the course as a whole, is unfair. It is also possible that the professor erred when calculating the grade. In these situations, first take a step back and review the comments and the numbers. If things do not add up or seem off, then craft a message. Here's an example:

> Dear Professor:
>
> I just received my final grade for Introduction to American Government and Politics. Although I received a B+ for every assignment, including the mid-term, my final grade was B. Can you help me understand how you arrived at that grade? Many thanks in advance for considering this matter. I look forward to hearing from you.

Being specific about your concern and asking for clarification can help you understand how the grade was calculated and if the facts support your case may result in a revision.

Assessing Your Own Performance

Here is a checklist that you can use to assess your own performance in an online class. Have I:

- ☐ Completed my institution's orientation to online learning?
- ☐ Read the syllabus carefully?
- ☐ Reviewed the assignments and noted their due dates?
- ☐ Signed into the course several times per week, preferably once every day?

- [ ] Introduced myself and made a strong effort to connect with my peers?

- [ ] Commented on the posts of my peers?

- [ ] Turned assignments in on time?

- [ ] Allocated enough time to complete assignments?

- [ ] Asked a peer to review my work?

- [ ] Allowed sufficient time to complete assignments?

- [ ] Done the assigned readings?

Going the extra mile. Great students ask themselves these additional questions. Have I:

- [ ] Sought outside sources to augment what I am reading in class, and brought the best articles to the attention of my classmates and professor?

- [ ] Gotten an outside opinion on my work?

- [ ] Demonstrated real interest in the topic by showing I know new literature in the field?

Takeaways

— Start early, review the course syllabus and learn about how your professor will evaluate your work.

— Keep track of your progress along the way, by using your institution's grade book. Tracking other details, such as how much time you spend in the course or the number of posts, can also shed light on performance.

— Feedback, in the form of comments and grades is one of the main ways that teaching happens online. Be open to learning from both your professor and your peers.

Chapter 9

Being a Great Online Student

We opened the book with how to get off to a strong start. In this chapter, we will explain what distinguishes a good online student from a great one and show you how you can go the extra mile to distinguish yourself in your online classes. Finally, we summarize key takeaways for savvy online students and suggest ideas for where you might go from here.

Characteristics of Great Online Students

By reading this book, you have already demonstrated a commitment to being a good online student. Great students go further. They exhibit tenacity, maintain motivation, know online netiquette, and, perhaps most importantly, are aware of their strengths and put them to work:

Tenacity. Obstacles are inevitable when you are in pursuit of something worthwhile. When learning online, you must embrace new tools, keep your motivation up, filter interruptions, and survive inevitable technical hiccups. Being an online student requires tenacity. Students are more likely to drop online courses than on-site ones. Still, the rewards are great. You can learn about a new subject, engage with experts and peers who share your passion for the subject matter, learn a new skill, or achieve mastery of a knowledge domain.

Motivation. Ask yourself why you decided to take an online class. How do you maintain your motivation?

Consider Brett Jones' MUSIC model, which breaks student motivation down into the following components: empowerment, usefulness, success, interest, and caring:

- Empowerment: Do you feel that you have the ability to make choices in your own learning?

- Usefulness: How does the content relate to your current and future goals?

- Success: Do you believe that you can succeed if you put in the effort?

- Interest: How interested are you in the subject? In learning online?

- Caring: How do your instructors feel about your progress toward the course's learning objectives? About you as a person?

Reflect upon these questions. The clearer you are about your answers, the stronger your motivation will be in an online course or program.

Effective communication. In earlier chapters, we discussed how written communication is often misunderstood. How can you be sure that you are getting your point across? One measure is whether or not others are responding to your ideas. Strive for clarity. Develop peer relationships so that you can ask for candid feedback on how you are doing at communicating. If you have a particularly important idea that you are trying to get across in your writing, consider writing a draft and sharing it with a friend or study buddy before posting. Schedule a phone call or Skype conversation to talk through your ideas. After the conversation, revise your post. Credit your peer in the post for helping you refine your thinking.

Netiquette. Larry Scheuermann and Gary Taylor surveyed the literature on how to be an effective participant in online conversations. Through their research, the following themes emerged:

- Write in lowercase—writing in upper case is akin to shouting.

- Limit abbreviations and emoticons—you may know exactly what you mean when you write AFAIK (as far as I know) but your peers may not. If your readers have to leave your post to Google an acronym, then you have taken their attention away from the ideas you are trying to get across.

- Refrain from flaming, taking offense easily or evangelizing—Flaming is writing that is designed to provoke others into a conflict. Don't do it. In a similar vein, given the limitations of written communication, try not to be easily offended.

- Consider all sides of an issue. Talking only about the merits of an idea or topic undermines your credibility. Be balanced. Introduce and address contradictory evidence. This approach strengthens your contributions and builds a reputation for being thoughtful.

Know your strengths. Peter Drucker, in a classic article entitled, "Managing Oneself," argues that many of us do not know what our strengths are, how we get things done or how we learn. His prescription for understanding these things? A technique he describes as "feedback analysis." Though Drucker had knowledge workers in mind, a consistent application of his approach will help you become a better student; namely someone who is more productive and makes more contributions to society. Self-knowledge is unique to you. Be an expert in yourself.

The feedback analysis technique is rather simple. When you embark on a new project, such as taking an online course, make notes about what you hope to achieve.

As the project progresses, check in on how you are doing in reaching the goals that you have established. How is your progress? What is working well? What could be better? How do you feel about your work? When the course is completed, ask yourself, what did you observe? When did you do your best work? Was it when you were solving a problem set on your own? Working through a thorny problem with a classmate? Helping lead a group discussion? Good learners are aware of how they learn. This process of being reflective about your work will reveal what you are good at.

Another technique to help discover your strengths is to ask your peers for stories about when you did your best work. This approach, pioneered by researchers Roberts, Dutton, Spreitzer, Heaphy, and Quinn, can be used to solicit anecdotes from a range of people to describe when you truly shined. Look for themes. Weave these anecdotes into a narrative to show when you are at your best.

Though we academics have a range of motivations for our career choices, it is safe to say that we have dedicated ourselves to continuous learning. Teaching others, and helping students become more expert in their subject areas is part of that process. Work on building professional relationships with your faculty. They can help guide your academic work, develop a talent you did not know you had and make introductions to others.

Active Participation in the Learning Process

Offer constructive feedback throughout the course. Students can influence the content and the pace of the course. For example, if you feel as though there's too much reading or not enough opportunity for practice in your course, you may want share this thought with your professor. The typical structure for feedback to the professor is a course evaluation. Evaluations are offered at, or near, the end of the semester. Although the comments may not help with the class you are currently taking, they will help future classes.

You may be fearful that if you criticize the class you could be hurting your grade: as in, "Yeah, I told Smithers his lectures put me to sleep, and then I got a C+ on my term paper. Next time I'll keep it under wraps." Though possible, and often the reason why evaluations are anonymous and given at the end of term, such outcomes are unlikely. If you offer thoughtful, constructive, and helpful feedback, you will not be penalized. Most instructors are eager to do a good job and hunger for perceptive insights that help them improve. Much of what we discussed earlier in Chapter 5 about constructive conversations also applies here.

When offering feedback, focus on something specific, that the professor can change: e.g.:

> I noticed that you added reading assignments in the middle of the week. I do most of my course work on the weekends, and it was almost impossible for me to read them before the class forum deadline, and as a result, I'm not as prepared as I'd like to be. Is there a way that they could be shared earlier, so that I can get the reading done? Can you let us know if they're optional?

Avoid making generalizations, such as:

> Your lectures are boring, and when they're not boring they're impenetrable. I get more from the textbook.

Instead, be specific:

> I got lost when you were explaining the first law of thermodynamics, and didn't want to stop class, because everyone seemed to be getting it. It might be helpful if you paused and asked one of us to explain the concept, instead of just asking if we've got it. I nod, but in truth, I am lost.

Thoughtful, honest feedback is likely to be heard by your professor.

Making a complaint. There may be times when it's appropriate to complain about the instructor to the department. Examples of situations that merit getting in touch with the department head include:

- Something important is missing—If key course materials are not there, for example, the course syllabus or an assignment and you have communicated your concerns to the faculty member but have not gotten a response.

- The instructor is unresponsive for an extended period of time—for example, he does not sign into the course, or does not provide feedback on assignments, or misses a session without explanation.

- The instructor humiliates or belittles a student or behaves erratically.

This list is not comprehensive—if you feel that something is not right, it is better to say something.

When writing a complaint, your email should be specific, state the concern, the consequences and the action you would like the professor, or department head, to take.

Here is an example of how to relay a concern to a faculty member. In this scenario, imagine that you and your peers have posted replies to a discussion assignment, but that you have not received any feedback.

Example Note to Faculty Member

Dear Professor McGill:

I am enjoying our History of Communications class; the readings are fascinating, and I am seeing how technologies that I have taken for granted shape our world. The discussion questions you post are also very engaging, and have sparked much debate—but we have not heard your perspective, or received a grade. The syllabus indicates that forum participation makes up 20 percent of our grade. I am concerned that we have not gotten any feedback or grades for those assignments. Could you let me know how and when they will be assessed? I also feel that your voice is missing, and could really help direct us. Perhaps I missed something—please let me know.

Sam Student

Make the Most of Your School's Resources

Your studies take place within the context of an educational institution. Academic work is collaborative, and requires research as well as administrative and technical support. When you begin your studies, take the time to learn about what your institution has to offer. You may be surprised. Most universities and colleges offer orientations and access to library resources:

Student orientations. Orientations help you get a sense of the range of services available to you. If your program offers an orientation just for online students, be sure to join it. You will learn about your institution's policies, the resources available to you, and have a chance to meet your peers.

Try it!

9.1 As part of this book, we've created a sample orientation for you to see what it's like to interact with others online in a learning context.

Student services and advising. Your institution is likely to offer advising services to help you find your way through an academic program. Advisors can offer insight into which courses to take and in what sequence and can help you connect courses to career paths. Student affairs' offices organize orientations and other events. Get to know what they offer.

Libraries. Depending upon whether or not you are in an online degree program, you may or may not have the pleasure of spending time in the library stacks, the section of the library where books are stored. Though more and more materials are available online, much of what is known about a topic resides in books. Libraries maintain subscriptions to research databases that are organized by field. Learn about the databases for your discipline and become familiar with ways to search them. Libraries are also staffed with librarians, who are there to help you. As Scott Collard, NYU's Librarian once quipped, "We're the only people who you can ask academic questions of without fear. We're not giving you a grade." Librarians can help point you toward the information you need to complete an assignment. Some libraries also have librarians available via live chat. Check to see if your institution does. If you are new to academic libraries, review Library Compass, a resource developed for students by Columbia University: http://ccnmtl.columbia.edu/projects/compass/. Your institution may have a similar introduction to its library services and academic research.

Writing center. Writing skills are developed over a lifetime. Earlier, we discussed how critical good writing is to online programs. Check to see if your school has a formal program to help students with writing. These centers can help you get structured feedback on drafts and become better writers. Even good writers benefit from having a colleague review their work.

Career services. Many institutions have groups dedicated to helping students make the transition from student to career professional, or assist with the transition from one career to another. These offices typically provide job listings and internship opportunities.

Center for student disabilities. These groups help level the playing field for students with disabilities who can participate in online learning experiences. For example, if key class elements are spoken, the student disability office may provide transcription or some other accommodation.

Help desk and technical support. We discussed gear at length in Chapter 2. If you are taking an online class, remember that it is not a question of if something will go wrong, but when. Don't pester your professor with technical questions. Call your institution's help desk instead.

Figure 9.1 Your online learning journey

Finish Strong

It may seem obvious, but as you near the course's end, return to the syllabus and make sure that you have submitted all assignments. Turn in any outstanding work. Next, check the course grade book and confirm that your instructor has posted your grades. If you discover that you have missed an assignment, or that your instructor has not graded an assignment, contact her. Consider this sample email:

Dear Professor Hu:

I just reviewed the grade book and noticed that I received a zero for the Week Three reflection. I went back and checked, and I did respond to that question, though I was a day late. Could you review my posting and update the grade book accordingly?

Best Regards,

Sue Anito (Classical Thought, CT-202)

Resolve such issues before the final date of the course. Though institutional requirements vary, instructors usually submit final grades within 3 to 5 days of the course's closing.

Evaluate the Course

Just as your instructor evaluates your performance and awards a final grade for the course, you will also have a chance to evaluate the instructor's teaching, and the course itself. As the term draws to a close, your professor, or a school representative, will ask you for your feedback (see Figure 9.2 for an example). Instructors and program directors rely upon data from these evaluations to improve courses, see how faculty are doing and assess student satisfaction. Chances are that you will be asked to reflect on the quality and relevance of course content, your professor's knowledge and instructional strategies, and on the learning environment itself. Some evaluations will ask you to reflect upon your own motivation, and even predict the grade you anticipate receiving.

Keep in mind:

- Most course evaluations are anonymous. Institutions keep this safeguard in place to encourage candid feedback and protect students from the fear of a possible reprisal.

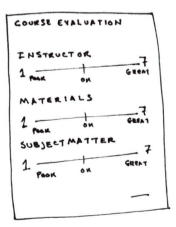

Figure 9.2 Course evaluation

- Instructors and your institution's staff will review your ratings and read your comments. Be thoughtful and constructive. Mean-spirited comments can hurt. Provide specific details about what helped your learning or what got in the way of it.

- Be aware that some institutions share anonymized student evaluations so that other students can make more informed choices about courses or sections.

Reflect on Your Own Learning

Once a course ends you, are freed from the burden associated with participating in it. Use found time to look back on what you learned. What did you learn about the subject? What did you notice about your interest? What did you learn about yourself? What do you think you did particularly well? What would you like to improve? How well did you manage your time? How effective were your contributions to team projects? How much effort did you exert?

Stay Connected to Colleagues and Professors

One of the benefits of studying online is the classroom is always open. After the course closes, you still may be able to view course materials and discussions, but you will not be able to add to them. How can you maintain the connections that you have made and keep the conversation going?

Savvy student strategy: use social networks with purpose.

Get a Recommendation, or Secure a Future Commitment for One

If you are at or near the end of your studies and you performed especially well in a course, consider asking your instructor for a recommendation. It will help if you are planning further study, or enrolling in a program that requires it. Application requirements vary from program to program, but it is best if you make the request,

Table 9.1 Social networks and when to use them

Facebook	LinkedIn	Twitter
Though mainly for social connections, you might find a relevant professional group that allows you and your classmates to keep the class conversation going.	Primary use is for professionals to establish connections to one another. There are many professional communities of practice. When extending a request to connect on LinkedIn, personalize the invitation. Endorse colleagues based on what they do particularly well. Avoid asking professors for LinkedIn endorsements; instead, ask for a recommendation letter.	Depends—mix of both. Simply following Twitter hashtags, e.g. #uspolitics, offers a way to join a conversation. You might even create a hashtag for your class, for example, eCommunities Fall 2012 might become #ecom2012. A more generic hashtag could facilitate interactions across different sections of the same class or past and present sections.

and then provide your professor's contact information to the institution that requires it. Keep the following points in mind when asking for a letter of recommendation:

- Professors are asked to write many such letters. Be clear on what the recommendation is for, why you want it, and why you think your professor is well positioned to write it.

- Provide detailed information about yourself that will make it easier for your professor to write the recommendation. Include the name of the class or classes you have taken together, the grades that you received, and what you see as your key contributions to the class.

- Make the request well before the program deadline. Make sure that you communicate the deadline to the professor after you secure an initial commitment for the recommendation.

- Offer an easy way out. For example, in your request to your professor say something like, "if, for any reason, you don't feel comfortable writing the recommendation letter, please do not feel obliged to do so."

Regardless of the response, thank your professor for considering your request. Thank her again once the reference letter has been submitted.

Join a Community of Practice

Knowledge, skills and experience reside not only in books and media, but in communities. By Wenger, McDermott, and Snyder's definition, a community of practice shares, "a concern, a set of problems, or passion about a topic, and deepens their knowledge and expertise in this area by interacting on an ongoing basis." These communities are filled with motivated individuals who do more than just contribute to the success of an organization. These knowledge centers and communities of practice generate, implement, and refine ideas.

You may already be a member of these communities. For example if you took a statistics course, you may have joined the R User Group after you downloaded the software. In your ongoing professional development, you may reference and use the resources created by the group. Perhaps you'll even contribute your knowledge as you gain expertise. Or for a data science course, you may have joined the Python Interest Groups (or "PIGgies") and attended a meet up with local members.

Professional associations are also great resources. For example, the Society of Human Resource Management's mission is to "ensure that HR is recognized as an essential partner in developing and executing organizational strategy" (www.shrm.org). Professional associations typically host conferences, meet ups, and provide job listings to their members. Keep learning by joining a community of practice.

Key Savvy Student Takeaways

Start Early, Start Strong

A good beginning in an online course generates momentum that propels you through the course. Sign in early, meet your peers and your professor, identify what is expected of you, develop a plan for your studies, and allocate more time than you think you will need. Establish regular, and deep patterns of participation in your online courses.

Contribute—Be Critical, Thoughtful, and Earnest

Logging into your class is only the beginning, once you are there, slow down, limit other possible digital distractions and focus on your work. Review assignments carefully. Make time to outline your thoughts before completing an assignment, whether thinking through how to solve an economics problem or engage in a debate about foreign affairs. Digital tools mediate your communication and body language and tone may be lost. Make an extra effort to be clear and kind.

Connect—with Your Professors and Peers, Before, During, and After the Course

Learning is a social process. Establish a professional online presence. The connections that you make with your peers and your professors support you on your journey as a learner. Still, developing these relationships takes time and effort. Be interested in others—ask good questions, be supportive and helpful. If you take this approach you will gain the respect of your faculty and peers.

Critique—Yourself, Your Peers, Your Instructor, Your Course, and the Program

Use your online studies to develop constructive critiques. Learn about what you do well and what your strengths are. Provide candid, yet helpful feedback in the right spirit. Solicit feedback from others. Apply it.

Continue—the Learning Never Stops

Learning is a lifelong process. Identify what you don't know, and what you need to know. Let your own interests and curiosity be your guide. Seek out meet ups, special interest groups, blogs, periodicals, and other resources that lead you to new areas to explore and learn.

Lifelong Learning Checklist

- ☐ Identify opportunities to develop or deepen skills or knowledge domains.

- ☐ Refine expand and share your expertise through joining communities of practice in your field or discipline.

- ☐ Exercise pro-active learning. Refer to books, the internet, and other resources.

- ☐ Ask questions.

- ☐ Network with others.

- ☐ Stay hungry to learn new things.

Takeaways

- ⁓ Assess and clarify your motivation for learning online.

- ⁓ Determine if you have enough time to study online.

- ⁓ Communicate clearly and effectively.

- ⁓ Engage in constructive confrontations.

- ⁓ Learn about what resources your school has to support your studies.

- ⁓ Provide constructive feedback to your professor.

Appendix A

Are You Ready to Take an Online Course?

We have a few questions for you.* Rather than a series of yes or no question, we've provided a scale for you to rate yourself.

1. How necessary is the course to your academic program or career?

Completely Unnecessary	Very Unnecessary	Somewhat Unnecessary	Neutral	Necessary	Very Necessary	Essential
1	2	3	4	5	6	7

The more you need to take the course, the more motivated you will be to succeed. See Chapter 1.

2. How skilled are you at managing your time?

Extremely Unskilled	Very Unskilled	Somewhat Unskilled	Neutral	Skilled	Very skilled	Extremely Skilled
1	2	3	4	5	6	7

Do you tend to put things off until the last minute, or do you get things done well ahead of time? Online classes demand consistent and frequent participation—sometimes even more than an on-site class. If you have problems with procrastination, online learning will be more difficult for you.

See Chapter 1.

---

* Palloff and Pratt, writing in *The Virtual Student* (2003, p. 162), developed an assessment to help gauge your readiness to learn online. We have updated their questions to be more contemporary.

3. How helpful are classroom discussions to your understanding of a topic?

Completely Unhelpful	Very Unhelpful	Somewhat Unhelpful	Neutral	Helpful	Very Helpful	Essential
1	2	3	4	5	6	7

Discussion tends to be a significant part of online classes. Discussions happen both in real time and in writing.

See Chapter 5.

4. How are your reading and writing skills?

Extremely Poor	Very Poor	Poor	Neutral	Good	Very Good	Excellent
1	2	3	4	5	6	7

You will be doing a fair amount of reading and writing online. You are expected to express yourself clearly in writing. Online courses offer a good forum to help you develop these skills.

5. How comfortable are you in asking for help when you need help understanding a subject?

Extremely Un-Comfortable	Very Un-Comfortable	Uncomfortable	Neutral	Comfortable	Very Comfortable	Extremely Comfortable
1	2	3	4	5	6	7

Students who do best online feel comfortable reaching out to their peers and their instructor.

See Chapter 4.

6. How would you describe your skill level in working with technological tools?

Extremely Un-Skilled	Very Unskilled	Somewhat Unskilled	Neutral	Skilled	Very Skilled	Extremely Skilled
1	2	3	4	5	6	7

When learning in an online program, all of your communication is mediated through some form. The ability to use it without paralyzing fear will help you succeed in an online class.

See Chapter 2.

7. Do you feel comfortable with the technologies necessary to be a successful online student?

Extremely Un-Comfortable	Very Un-Comfortable	Uncomfortable	Neutral	Comfortable	Very Comfortable	Extremely Comfortable
1	2	3	4	5	6	7

Interactions in an online course require various types of technological knowledge that enable you to participate in the learning experience. Because you will be asked to access a variety of systems, consider your technological experience from several angles.

8. How well do you use web-based tools to communicate, collaborate, and access research databases?

Extremely Poor	Very Poor	Poor	Neutral	Good	Very Good	Excellent
1	2	3	4	5	6	7

You may feel comfortable sending and reading emails, but have you ever communicated online using instant messaging, discussion forums, or a web conferencing tool?

You may use the internet to search for information, but have you ever used internet databases to conduct academic research?

See Chapters 4 and 5.

How Did You Rate?

If you answer with mostly 6s or 7s they you can see that you are well prepared to take an online course. If you scored lower on some questions, they involve some challenges you can overcome and improve. Each question is covered in one or more chapters in the book. Try reading about the specific issues that are most important to you.

Appendix B

When Technology Fails

Technologies are pretty much guaranteed to fail. Don't panic when things go wrong. Be prepared and anticipate where problems can happen.

Try the following steps in this order when you're having a problem:

1. Try logging out, closing your browser window and signing back on, if that doesn't work then . . .

2. Quit out of your browser completely, and then try signing back in, if that doesn't work then . . .

3. Try another browser. Using Firefox? Try Safari? On Internet Explorer? Try Chrome instead. You've made sure they're up to date, well before class right?

4. Restart your computer. We avoid taking this step—it seems time consuming. It has the effect of shutting down programs that may be in conflict with one another. You thought siblings and countries were the only entities that fought? Guess what, your computer's got programs that are fighting for limited resources. The restart levels the virtual playing field. Still not working?

5. Make sure everything is plugged in. It sounds ridiculous right? Still, check and make sure that your network cable is securely attached. On a wireless network? Turn that router off and turn it back on again.

6. Call your school's help desk. Be prepared to tell them:

   a. The course you're trying to access. For example: "Hi, my name is Tina Reyes, I'm a student in the eCommunities course at NYU. I am trying to access our live session, which starts in 30 minutes."

b. The kind of computer you're using, and what operating system: "I'm on a Dell Inspiron, running Windows 7."

c. The browser you're using. Example: "I am using Internet Explorer 9. I also tried Firefox version 14. No luck."

d. The steps you took to solve the problem: "I signed out, signed back in, and even restarted my computer."

e. The specific error message you're getting: "When I try to sign into the Live Classroom, I get a 'J Secure Door 40' error."

f. Let the tech guide you to resolve the problem. If they can't find a solution, they'll get you to someone who can.

g. At peak times, you might experience a longer wait. Take advantage of the call back option if it's offered.

h. For live online classes, if your institution has a way to "dial in" instead of using your computer, use this option for class. Be sure to mute your phone's microphone before you dial in. Unmute it to participate in class.

Bibliography

Arum, R., & Roksa, J. (2011). *Academically Adrift: Limited Learning on College Campuses*. Chicago, IL: University of Chicago Press.

Babson Survey Research Group. (2011). New Study: Over 6 million Students Learning Online. 9 November. Retrieved February 12 from www.babson.edu/News-Events/babson-news/Pages/111109 OnLineLearningStudy.aspx.

Betts, K. (2009). Lost in Translation: Importance of effective communication in online education. *Online Journal of Distance Learning Administration*, 12 (2).

Brown, J. S., & Adler, R. (2008). Minds on fire: Open education, the long tail, and learning 2.0. *Educause Review*, 43 (1).

Dante, E. (2010). The shadow scholar. *The Chronicle of Higher Education*. November 12.

Drucker, P. F. (2005). Managing oneself. *Harvard Business Review*, 83 (1), 1009.

Elder, L., Paul, R., & Hiler, W. (2001). *Thinker's Guide Series*. Dillon, CA: Foundation for Critical Thinking.

Hansen, M. (2009). *Collaboration: How Leaders Avoid Traps, Create Unity, and Reap Big Results*. Boston, MA: Harvard Business Press.

Hiltz, S. R., & Goldman, R. (2005). *Learning Together Online: Research on Asynchronous Learning Networks*. New York: Routledge.

Illinois Online Network. (n.d.). Educational resources. Retrieved August 27, 2012, from www.ion.uillinois.edu/resources/tutorials/pedagogy StudentProfile.asp.

Jones, B. D. (2010). An examination of motivation model components in face-to-face and online instruction. *Electronic Journal of Research in Educational Psychology*, 8 (38), 915–944.

Kruger, J., Epley, N., Parker, J., & Ng, Z. W. (2005). Egocentrism over e-mail: Can we communicate as well as we think? *Journal of Personality and Social Psychology*, 89 (6), 925–936.

Mayer, R. E. (2005). *The Cambridge Handbook of Multimedia Learning*. New York: Cambridge University Press.

Middle States Commission on Higher Education. (2009). Degrees and credits. Retrieved September 29, 2012, from www.msche.org/documents/Degree-and-Credit-Guidelines-062209-FINAL[1].pdf.

Mindtools. (2012). Team charters: Getting your teams off to a great start. Retrieved January 15, 2012, from Mindtools: www.mindtools.com/pages/article/newTMM_95.htm.

Osterhof, A., Conrad, R., & Ely, D. (2007). *Assessing Learners Online*. New York: Pearson.

Palloff, R. M., & Pratt, K. (2003). *The Virtual Student: A Profile and a Guide to Working with Online Learners*. San Francisco, CA: Jossey-Bass.

Patterson, K., Grenny, J., McMillan, R., & Switzler, A. (2008). *Crucial Conversations Tools for Talking When Stakes Are High*. New York: McGraw-Hill.

Pentland, A. (2012, April). The new science of building great teams: The chemistry of high-performing groups is no longer a mystery. *Harvard Business Review*.

Pratt, R. M., & Palloff, K. (2005). *Collaborating Online: Learning Together in Community*. San Francisco, CA: Jossey-Bass.

Roberts, L., Dutton, J., Spreitzer, G., Heaphy, E., & Quinn, R. (2005). Composing the reflected best self portrait: Building pathways for becoming extraordinary in work organizations. *Academy of Management Review*, 30 (4), 712–736.

Roper, A. (2007). How students develop online learning skills. *Educause Quarterly*. January 1.

Ryan, M. (2010). Leadership. In R. Ubell, *Virtual Teamwork: Mastering the Art and Practice of Online Learning and Corporate Collaboration*. Hoboken, NJ: John Wiley & Sons.

Scheuermann, L., & Taylor, G. (1997). Netiquette. *Internet Research*, 7 (4), 269–273.

Scollins-Mantha, B. (2008). Cultivating social presence in an online classroom: A literature review with recommendations for practice. *International Journal of Instructional Technology and Distance Learning*, 5 (3).

Teaching and Learning with Technology at Penn State. (2011). Getting started with Unicode. Retrieved June 13, 2012, from Computing with access, symbols, and foreign scripts: http://tlt.its.psu.edu/suggestions/international/web/unicode.html.

Tuckman, B., & Jensen, M. (1977). Stages of small group development revisited. *Group and Organizational Studies*, 2 (4), 419–427.

Vai, M., & Sosulsk, K. (2011). *The Essentials of Online Course Design: A Standards Based Guide*. New York: Routledge.

Volchok, E. (2010). Building virtual teams. In R. Ubell, *Virtual Teamwork: Mastering the Art and Practice of Online Learning and Corporate Collaboration*. Hoboken, NJ: John Wiley & Sons.

Wenger, E., McDermott, R., & Snyder, W. M. (2002). *Cultivating Communities of Practice*. Cambridge, MA: Harvard Business School Publishing.

Index